# Edgar Cay)
## Guide tᴏ
## Gemstones,
## Minerals,
## Metals,
## and More

# Edgar Cayce Guide to Gemstones, Minerals, Metals, and More

Shelley Kaehr, Ph.D.

A.R.E. Press • Virginia Beach • Virginia

A.R.E. Press
215 67th Street
Virginia Beach, VA 23451-2061


Library of Congress Cataloguing-in-Publication Data
Kaehr, Shelley, 1967-.
Edgar Cayce guide to gemstones, minerals, metals, and more / Shelley Kaehr
p.   cm.
Includes bibliographical references.
ISBN 0-87604-503-4 (trade pbk.)
ISBN 13: 978-0-87604-503-9
1. Precious stones–Psychic aspects  2. Precious stones–Therapeutic use.  3. Minerals–Psychic aspects  4. Minerals–Therapeutic use.  5. Metals–Psychic aspects.  6. Metals–Therapeutic use.  I. Title.
BF1442.P74K34 2005
133'.2549–dc22

                                        2005001848

**A Note to the Reader**

The thoughts and opinions expressed in this book are those of the author and do not necessarily reflect the medical or metaphysical philosophy of the Edgar Cayce readings or the policy of the A.R.E.

Edgar Cayce gave readings for particular individuals with specific conditions; therefore, no part of this book is intended as medical advice, nor does the A.R.E. endorse any of the information contained herein as prescription for the treatment of disease.

**A Note About the Cayce Readings**

During Edgar Cayce's life, the Cayce psychic readings were all numbered to provide confidentiality. The first set of numbers (e.g., "294") refers to the individual or group for whom the reading was given. The second set of numbers (e.g., "5") refers to the number in the series from which the reading is taken. For example, 294-5 identifies the reading as the fifth one given to the subject assigned #294.

Cover design by Richard Boyle

# Contents

**Part Three: Gems, Stones, and Minerals**

# Acknowledgments

As with any project of this magnitude, there are many people to thank. First, to my great friends Dr. Raymond Moody and Auda Marie, thank you for introducing me to the A.R.E. and for supporting my work.

To Charles Thomas Cayce, Leslie Cayce, and Ken Skidmore, thank you for your support and for commissioning me to do this project.

To my many friends in the gem business, including: Charlie and Pat Mark, Steven "Crystalmaster" Rosley, Gary Fleck, Kayse Williams, Katchie Stewart, Bob Nelson, and Gary Kaufman, who have taught me so much.

To the many gracious people who allowed me to photograph their stones and told me wonderful tales of the gem trade, I am deeply grateful. Thanks to Jimmy and Joyce Cacek, Neil Kinnane, Bob and Mary Lewis, Jacky Chan, Sandy and Trudy Craig, Theo Manos and Demetrios Constantinades, Anthony Frasier, Pat and Kathy Curry, Marc Jobin, Ken Allgier, Mike and Sandra Sprunger, and Rolfe Foxwell.

To my friends for their love and support: Paul Martin, Joe Crosson, Gordon Morehead, Linnea Armstong, Cheryl Doyle, Kathy Brown, Michelle Burden, Victoria Wong, Lori Edwards, and Nancy Zak.

And finally to my family: Mickey, Gail, and Mark, without you I would not be able to write and I would know nothing about gems and minerals. I THANK YOU!

# Introduction

One night, a few years ago, I had a dream that I was being led down a dimly lighted tunnel with earthen walls. I followed the path and came upon a large open room where the figure of a man stood with his back to me.

As the man turned around and I saw his face, I was stunned. It was Edgar Cayce. Although his eyes were open, he appeared trancelike as he spoke but a single phrase to me: *The Maltese Falcon.*

I gasped, and that motion alone was enough to startle me out of my deep sleep. I replayed the sequence hundreds of times in my mind over the next few days, wondering what it meant.

I walked to the library first thing the next morning to retrieve a copy of Dashiell Hammett's classic and began to read. It would take many months for me to finally figure out the significance of the book to my own path, and now the novel is indelibly engrained in my consciousness forever.

Shortly after that, I began having a recurring dream about a beautiful beach I had never been to before. The serenity and beauty of it was unlike any I had ever seen. I grew up in California and North Carolina and wondered where this beach was since it was clearly not those places, nor any I had seen in Florida, or elsewhere in the world.

Within a couple of months, I was at my parent's house while they were watching a program on television featuring a segment on Virginia Beach.

When I saw the long misty stretches of sand and the beautifully peaceful white buildings, I immediately recognized it as the place I visited in my dream. Still, I had yet to discover what it all meant.

A few years ago, I wrote a book called *Gemstone Journeys* to teach people about my experiences in gem healing. Each year since then I travel to the Tucson Gem and Mineral Show to sign a few books, see friends and purchase minerals.

My annual trip across the desert is like a pilgrimage to me now. It is a time for me to journey alone and reflect on the previous year, while planning the future.

During last year's trip, I was guided to take along the book *Gems and Stones Based on the Edgar Cayce Readings*, originally compiled by the A.R.E. in 1960. I somehow knew I was to begin to explore some of the gems and stones Cayce spoke about in the life readings by purchasing and working with them.

That is one of the things I love most about this topic. No matter how many years you live, there is always so much more to learn. The mineral kingdom is so vast; I doubt it is possible to explore it all in just one lifetime. I certainly intend to try.

After my desert journey, I was clearly guided to approach the A.R.E. about updating this material, and it is my great honor to do so.

I have always admired Edgar Cayce's work, not only because of his immense talents as a psychic, but because of the man himself.

I am inspired by Cayce's story of hardship and perseverance. No matter what happened he knew what God sent him here to do and did whatever was necessary to live life according to His purpose. For that, Cayce is a hero in my mind.

In these next pages, we will explore one of my favorite topics as it relates to the greatest psychic to ever live—Edgar Cayce.

# Part One
# Vibrational Healing

# 1

# Fundamentals of Energy Medicine

As is known, the body in action or a live body—emanates from same the vibrations to which it as a body is vibrating, both physical and spiritual. Just as there is an aura when a string of a musical instrument is vibrated—the tone is produced by the vibration. In the body the tone is given off rather in the higher vibration, or the color. Hence this is a condition that exists with each physical body.                    440-6

would like to begin by explaining some of the fundamentals of energy or vibrational healing. As you know, everything in the universe is made up of basically the same things—strings of atoms put together in millions of different ways. Ancient Hawaiians believed you are really no different from the chair you are sitting on, meaning everything has consciousness, of some sort. What separates you and me from our kitchen table is the carbon element, which gives us life and soul.

When you are born, you are in essence a perfect creation of the Almighty.

You would think, then, since you are created in His image, that you would be able to live a beautiful, peaceful life filled with joy and love, right?

The problem with that scenario is that if you were to have a "perfect life," you would not have the amazing opportunities to learn and grow, which is why we came here in the first place.

To believe in past lives says that you come here again and again to evolve as a soul and to gain different types of experiences. That is why we are often born with all kinds of blockages or challenges to overcome.

Sometimes these challenges affect our physical body through health issues, or they can arise in emotional traumas.

## The Seven Chakras

(Q) How may I bring into activity my pineal and pituitary glands, as well as the Kundalini and other chakras, that I may attain to higher mental and spiritual powers?

(A) As indicated, first so *fill* the mind with the ideal that it may vibrate throughout the whole of the *mental* being! Then, close the desires of the fleshly self to conditions about same. *Meditate* upon *"Thy will with me."* Feel same. Fill *all* the centers of the body, from the lowest to the highest, with that ideal; opening the centers by surrounding self first with that consciousness, "Not my will but Thine, O Lord, be done in and through me."

And then, have that desire, that purpose, not of attaining without *His* direction, but *with* His direction—who is the Maker, the Giver of life and light; as it is indeed in Him that we live and move and have our being.     1861-4

In Eastern thought, it is believed the body has seven primary energy centers called chakras. These chakras are located at various points within the physical body, and although you cannot see them with your physical eyes, they exist in the form of swirling vortexes that would look like colored funnel or tornado clouds, each one representing a different color in the rainbow spectrum.

In the ideal situation, all seven of these energy centers are open and functioning at their maximum capacity. Usually, though, that is not always the case. Each blocked chakra helps to create the lessons you have come here to learn.

The chakra centers are as follows:

### First Chakra
### Root
### Color: Red

The first or root chakra, located at the base of the spine, connects you with the earth. It is the oldest, most primitive part of you, determined to survive. It is about your basic needs of food, clothing, and shelter. Blockages in this area make it difficult to manifest life's most basic necessities.

### Second Chakra
### Sacral
### Color: Orange

The second chakra, located just below the naval, is called the sacral. It is about sexual energy, the process of creation, and your ability to manifest abundance. Abundance is a word that means different things to different people. For one person, it may mean having a nice car to drive or wearing nice clothes, while for others it might mean having enough to eat and a roof over their heads. The lessons of the second chakra deal with the ability to manifest these things on the physical plane. Abundance is not just a feeling of having enough, but also it is a physical expression of what you have manifested, like that new car, for example. It is the difference between daydreaming about something and actually doing what it takes to go out and get it. It is about material manifestation. Creation is also ruled by this center—your ability to create things from scratch whether that's a new art project or having a baby.

Blockages in this area could lead to creative blocks, poor finances, or health problems in the reproductive areas.

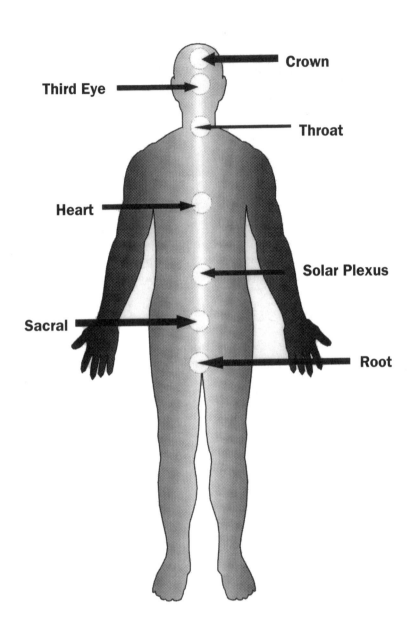

Crown

Third Eye

Throat

Heart

Solar Plexus

Sacral

Root

*Chakra Chart*

### Third Chakra
### Solar Plexus
### Color: Yellow

The third chakra is located where your two ribs join right below your breastbone. The solar plexus chakra is all about your power and your ability to stand up for yourself and how secure you feel in the world on more of a mental level, than in the survival mode of the root chakra center.

You may have suffered from stomach problems in your lifetime, or you know someone who has. It is a very common ailment, particularly in the world we now live in where power and greed too often prevail. Blockages in this area mean you are having a hard time facing things, or standing your ground. Another, perhaps even bigger problem facing our society today stems from an overactive solar plexus, which causes greed, lack of feeling or regard for others, and ruthlessness. The key to it all is balance.

### Fourth Chakra
### Heart
### Color: Green

You may be surprised to learn the color of the heart chakra is green and not pink, but it really makes a lot of sense. Green is the color of life and of growth. In the springtime when the new flowers bloom and the grass begins to grow after a long winter, the feeling of renewal can make your heart sing. The biggest challenge facing mankind today is to learn the lessons of the heart. To learn to love and express our feelings in the face of fear of rejection or heartache is a continual challenge. Love is the reason why you are here. It is something I think we are getting better at, but there is still a long way to go.

As you may imagine, blockages in the heart center cause all kinds of health problems including heart attack, stroke, and blocked or crooked arteries. Emotionally, they can cause people to be cold, unfeeling, or withdrawn.

### Fifth Chakra
### Throat
### Color: Light Blue

Each chakra center opens as you learn the lessons of that particular area, like a ladder; the lessons get more and more difficult as you move toward the top. Once the heart is opened up, then the lessons of the throat can begin. This is one of the most difficult to master of all. The throat center is all about how you express yourself to the world. Do you hold back your true feelings, worrying about getting in trouble or upsetting someone, or are you able to tell people, with compassion, how you really feel and not be afraid to do so? With all of the pressure in our society to be "politically correct," this one is tough!

Blockages in this area can cause all kinds of problems both physically and emotionally. Cancers, nervous tremors, thyroid conditions, and gum diseases can all result from the frustration of feeling unable to express yourself. Emotionally, these blockages can also cause extreme shyness or withdrawal or stuttering.

### Sixth Chakra
### Third Eye
### Color: Violet/Indigo Blue

Have you ever wanted to see the future or to be able to read people like a book? These are the gifts of the third eye. Edgar Cayce said himself that this is something anyone can do with practice. I believe that in past lives we used these gifts freely and without criticism and that you can learn to do it again by simply remembering how it is done. Many of the stones you will learn about later in the book will help you open up to intuitive guidance.

Blockages in this area can cause life to be difficult. You may find yourself running into walls by not listening to the tiny voice within. These can also cause headaches and strain on the physical eyes.

### Seventh Chakra
### Crown
### Color: White

The seventh chakra center is the one that will connect you with your

Creator and makes you feel loved and knowing of an eternal bliss to which you connected at all times. The Greeks believed when you incarnate that you agree to dip into a river of forgetfulness so that when you arrive here, you won't remember all you already know and can come here to learn and wake up to all your gifts. The crown center provides that very subconscious link to the all that is in the universe that makes you feel connected to everything.

Blockages in this area will cause severe melancholy and depression. Manic depression is caused by a continual flux between an underactive or blocked crown to an overactive or overly opened crown which causes the unpredictable depressive dips and extreme bliss.

# Energetic Bodies

Now that you have the basics of the chakras, there is another area we need to cover briefly I call the subtle energy system, or energetic bodies.

You and I are connected with everything in the universe, and now, besides just considering that statement as a new age mantra, legitimate scientists are actually beginning to prove its true.

You have hundreds of energetic fields around your body. Haven't you noticed how sad you feel when you hear someone died you don't even know? Or you may feel overwhelmed with joy when you see an athlete at the Olympics winning a medal. It is as if you can feel what they feel, to a certain degree. There is a part of you that is connected to everyone at a very subtle level, which is why you feel that way.

It would be hard to imagine the vastness of these energetic fields, so for the sake of simplicity, let's say they consist of three layers: the astral, mental, and causal.

### Astral Layer

The astral layer is the energetic field closest to your body. If there are any energetic blockages, those in this layer will be the first to affect your body and health. This layer is about the physical body.

### Mental Layer

The mental layer is similar to the first, second and third chakra cen-

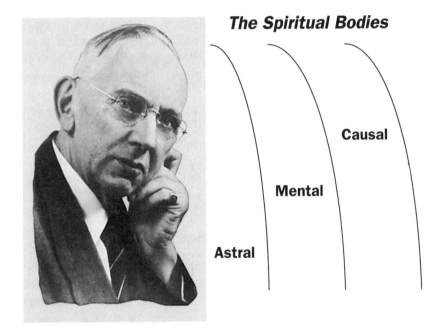

## The Spiritual Bodies

Causal

Mental

Astral

ters. It is about manifestation and creation, and as the term mental would suggest, the emotions. Blockages here could affect your material abundance and your survival, and it is here where you may be holding on to old feelings of anger, sadness, fear, or guilt.

### Causal Layer

The causal is another word for spiritual. This layer is actually the never-ending part of you that goes beyond the emotional and third dimensional reality and connects you to the universe. Opening this area will bring you deep feelings of centeredness and peace.

# 2

# Vibrational Healing Basics

*Hence we find these as those things that should be in the form of omens about the body; not as good luck charms, but they may be termed so by many; for these are from those activities and sojourns that will make for variations in the* vibrations *about the entity, hence bringing much more of harmony into the experience of the entity in the present activity.* 694-2

There is a theory that there is a hologram of you lying outside of your physical body. It is like a blueprint of how you would be if you were in perfect health and had no blockages at all. Scientists now know you can store memories holographically around your body and those memories are lying somewhere out in the energetic bodies I have just described.

This is particularly true of emotions. Illness is driven, much of the time, by our emotions. Energy work, or vibrational medicine, works to open up your energy centers, and release, transform, and heal the emotional memory holograms from your energy field so you have more life force to use on constructive purposes and you will feel much better.

# How Gem Healing Works

If you have been familiar with Edgar Cayce and his psychic discourses for any amount of time, you know the importance he placed on "the vibrations." This term is mentioned over 2500 times in his readings. Cayce eloquently explained the nature of vibration in the following reading:

> We know that all force is created by vibration. We know that all vibration becomes electrical in its action and its effect. That is, it either enlivens, bring greater vibration, or being under vibration becomes deadened or destructive to one or the other of the vibrations thus met.
>
> **2492-5**

Cayce knew, even then, about all of the things everybody else is just now starting to realize—that you and I are made up of the same stuff as everything else in the universe. That means it should be obvious you are going to be influenced and affected by everything around you.

You are affected by the foods you eat, the clothes you wear, your living arrangements, your friends and people you associate with—everything—because all of these things have different vibrations and some will help you while others can harm you.

The readings continually go over ways to increase, assist, or stabilize vibrations. Each person is different, and Cayce knew that, so he would sometimes offer totally different suggestions to people suffering the same illness because he could read their vibrations and tell what would work best in any given circumstance.

In this book, you will have a chance to explore many of these readings and remedies and use your own intuitive abilities to decide what feels best to you and what you think will work. You will empower yourself to heal, learn a lot, and hopefully have some fun in the process.

When you change your vibration, you change everything, as demonstrated in the following reading:

> (Q) This will eradicate also the breaking out on the skin, Mr. Cayce?
> (A) Yes, the change of vibration, or change of forces in the system, will change these conditions in the body.  2722-1

When you begin to experiment with the different minerals in this book, you will start to see energetic shifts occur within your body. Any condition, whether emotional or physical, has to change when you change your vibration.

Once you understand that your body is vibrating at a particular frequency, you begin to realize that for any illness to be held there, or any negative emotion to stay with you, it must have an energetic counterpart that is somewhere in your energetic bodies.

The metals, gems, and stones you will read about in this book each have unique properties and unique vibrations about them. All you have to do is find one that will help you with what you need to transform.

I am convinced there are only three things we all want in this world: (1) Love, (2) Health, and (3) Security—either financial or emotional. Everything in life can simply be broken down to one of these three categories. Not to belittle or oversimplify the complexities in which you live, but really, when you think about it, that is about all there is, and even the life readings reflect that because they are just about always concerning one of these three topics.

Each one of the items you will see in this book holds a vibrational frequency that will align you in one of these three areas. Depending on what it is you need to attract—health, love, or money—you can find something in the book to help you do that.

In gem healing, you will be bringing the stone, gem, or metal into your own energetic field—into your subtle energy system, or you will place the stone on one or more of your chakra centers.

When you do that, because your body is very responsive, your energy system will begin to emulate or imitate the vibrations being given off by the item you work with.

When you begin to change your vibration to match the gem, stone, or metal, you will attract to yourself the same things the gem or stone attracts to it. It is really very simple and yet very profound at the same time.

## Cleansing and Caring for Your Stones

This leads to an interesting point—just like you have an energetic field around you, so do your stones. That is why they need to be cleansed.

I mentioned earlier in the book that you have various energy fields around you. Stones are no different. Everything in the universe has a hologram around it.

When you handle stones or minerals, they will pick up energy from you by taking on some of your patterns in order to help you heal. When this happens, it is necessary to cleanse them.

By far, the best and easiest way to clean your stones is by taking them outside and putting them on the ground. It is very powerful to put the stones in the light of the full moon to cleanse and charge them, or you can put them in the sun. Be careful, though, if you live in a very hot place like I do because bright sunlight will permanently fade and damage some stones, such as amethyst, fluorite, and carnelian. It is best on very hot days to put the stones out under your plants or trees out of direct light.

When you put them on the ground outside, the energetic patterns they are holding will get dispersed in the earth and transformed to a more productive state. Just like fertilizers are negatives that help the plants grow, I have seen stones with negative vibrations used to help plants grow, too, just by putting them outside underneath the plants or trees for clearing. It is really amazing to see.

Later in the book I will talk about the different kinds of salts that are also great to use for cleaning.

## A Word on Good Luck Charms and Talismans

Ye are interested in seeking things—things unusual. Thus

> the study of those things that man has found will bring
> certain results when used in this routine or in that type of
> activity. These can only bring so much power as ye as an
> individual give to such things. For ye are a co-creator with
> thy God.                                                           3285-2

In the next section you will begin to take a look first at all of the
elements, metals, and non-metals found in nature, then you will explore the many wonders of the mineral kingdom.

Before you begin, I want to mention one more important thing. As
you look at the entries and learn what each element or mineral can do,
remember what Cayce himself tried to teach us—that you are a totally
unique creation and what works for someone else may or may not
work for you. It is all based on the complexities of your soul, your
akashic record, and the lessons you came here to learn this time around.
Let the book be a guideline to you to help in your own exploration of
self and through that, you will find the stones, minerals, or elements
that are right for you to use.

Toward the end of the book, you will have an opportunity to travel
to a place where you will learn which ones are best for you at this time.
You will also learn how to give an energy session to yourself and others,
after you learn about all of the elements, gems, and minerals.

Aside from the physical or vibrational reasons why stone and mineral healing works, there is a mental part to it also that is tied to your
thoughts and consciousness.

Cayce was adamant about making sure the stones he recommended
were not seen as "talismans," or "good luck charms," as in the following
reading:

> We find that the crystal as a stone, or any white stone, has
> a helpful influence—if carried about the body; not as an
> omen, not merely as a "good luck piece" or "good luck
> charm" but these vibrations that are needed as helpful
> influences for the entity are well to be kept close about
> the body.                                                          2285-1

I'm sure Cayce warned people against thinking of these as charms because if you were to get to the point of believing in this stone so much that you thought you couldn't live without it, that would not be very productive. The stone will help you because of vibrations, and if you believe it will, yet you do not need to become dependent on it, or on any other material possession.

You have probably heard about the Hope Diamond and the alleged curse that befalls its owners. While it is true that energetic blue prints can hold on to objects, do you really believe the stone is cursed, or did the owners just happen to come on hard times and erroneously attribute them to the Hope?

You always get what you think about, and because of that, if you think something will help you get better, it will. The contrary, as in the case of the Hope Curse, is also true. That is the amazing power of the mind, at its best! Together, your body/mind is like an incredible machine just waiting to be programmed to do exactly what you ask.

There is an interesting reading about a turquoise ring. The original owner gave it away on her deathbed to her good friend, but the friend felt bad because the ring was too big for her to wear so she gave it to her other friend who had admired it for some time. Disaster struck quickly because the new owner had complications each time she put the ring on; so this, and other things, led her to Cayce for a life reading. In a letter written on October 28, 1946, she reported, in hindsight, about what happened to her when she wore the ring:

> Within a few days my finger became inflamed and itchy under the stone. Of course I removed it until it was well and then put on the ring again. After a few days the same condition returned and lasted until I took off the ring. I tried again and again to wear it but always with the same result.     4009-1 Reports

Cayce gave her a reading and she asked about the stone and what could be causing the irritation:

> (Q) Why does my little finger break out when I wear a certain ring?

> (A) The super-sensitiveness of the body to vibrations of this particular ring—from those vibrations that are a part of the ring.                                    4009-1

One could speculate that this ring is "cursed," or haunted by the deceased owner who wanted her other friend to keep the ring. Or we can just assume that for whatever reason, the stone was not vibrationally compatible to the new owner. Either way, it is all in how you perceive it.

Minerals and stones will serve you by acting as a tool for your unconscious mind that will represent whatever outcome or healing you desire. You have the power within you to heal yourself from head to toe. All you need are the proper tools.

Let's get ready now to start the journey into self-discovery and healing.

# Part Two
# The Elements

# Metals and Non-Metals

For within the human body—living, not dead—*living* human forces—we find every element, every gas, every mineral, every influence that is outside of the organism itself. For indeed it is one with the whole.                470-022

Hence we find, because the activities of the entity through the earth have involved and do involve the lives and activities of the many, the elements that are of nature's vibrations would have, do have, much to do with the entity's activity.                2073-2

When you consider the amazing world we live in, it is sometimes hard to imagine everything you see around you is all composed of the 120 elements in the periodic table.

Cayce mentioned these elements so often in the readings, which should come as no surprise, because they truly are the building blocks not only of our world but of the known universe.

In the next section you will explore many readings about these forces of nature and what Cayce had to say about them.

# Metals

As will be, as has been the experience, days and periods the vibrations from metals and their elements have a great deal of influence upon the entity.          1580-1

## *Aluminum*
### Al
### Atomic Number 13

### History

Aluminum is a metal obtained from the mineral bauxite, which was discovered in Les Baux, France, in 1827 by Hans Christian Oersted.

Aluminum is a pure white metal with high reflectivity which means that most of the light that shines on it is returned to the viewer, a result of the light color. In its natural state, it is one of the hardest metals and is one of the most abundant of all the elements in the earth's crust.

Pure aluminum is an excellent conductor for electricity, and aluminum wire was previously used in home building until it was discovered to be a potential fire hazard because of the way the element oxidizes, or reacts to oxygen. Other commercial uses range from foil to automobile spark plugs to cosmetics.

The crystalline state of aluminum is called corundum, known in the mineral kingdom as rubies and sapphires, both of which will be explored later in the book. There are many other minerals containing aluminum including turquoise, lapis lazuli, and sodalite.

In healing, aluminum can be used externally to assist severe circulation problems such as gout by wrapping aluminum foil around the feet and legs, and arms if applicable. The conductivity of the foil assists with the electrical flow of the body.

### Cayce Uses

Aluminum is mentioned 153 times in 102 documents in the Cayce readings, proving it was considered to be an important element. Many of the readings talk about various recipes and remedies and warn people to avoid internal exposure to aluminum.

Today there is concern about the link between Alzheimer's disease and aluminum, particularly because aluminum is so abundant and impossible for us to avoid. Current daily intake for the average person is about 30–50 mg per day from foods, drinking water, and pharmaceuticals. Many food additives contain aluminum, particularly those in cheese.

Although the Alzheimer's Association recently reported that there is no certain link between high aluminum exposures and the disease, a recent study suggests that cooking highly acidic foods such as tomatoes in aluminum pans causes 3–5 mg of aluminum to be present for each 100g serving. Such trace amounts as these should not cause concern if it were not for the cumulative effects of the exposure over time.

During Cayce's lifetime, Alzheimer's disease was virtually unknown. German physician Dr. Alois Alzheimer told colleagues about a woman under his care in 1901, who suffered an unusual form of dementia. This 1910 presentation was the first time the disease was ever mentioned, and the research that followed ultimately led to the identification of the disease bearing his name.

Alzheimer's is not mentioned at all in any of the readings, yet Cayce clearly knew of a danger of high aluminum exposure and even cited the fact that the hazard has to do with what kind of food was being served. Once again, Cayce was ahead of his time.

Cayce also recommends many of the aluminum–based gemstones in the readings mentioned later in the book. Aluminum based gems allow the soul to move into higher spiritual realms and remember talents and spiritual abilities from past lives. Aluminum allows us to access higher realms of consciousness by breaking the sound barrier between our world and the spirit world so it is easier to hear spirit guides.

### Sample Aluminum Readings

(Q) Are aluminum cooking vessels a detriment to health?
(A) To some; and dependent upon what's cooked in 'em!
340-31

Mornings—alternate between fresh fruits with cereal, or citrus fruit or whole wheat—the wheat that is rolled, but cooked at least for an hour or hour and a half; and this means cooking *covered*, not in aluminum but rather in enamel or glassware. *Not* in aluminum. For with this condition, aluminum becomes poisonous to the system. Do not use aluminum ware in *any* form where this body takes food from!                                              1223-1

# *Barium*
## Ba
## Atomic Number 56

### History

Carl Wilhelm Scheele first discovered barium oxide in 1774, but it was not separated from its ore until Sir Humphrey Davy did so in 1808, so Davy is credited with the discovery. It is used in electronics, spark plugs, fireworks, rocket fuels, and most commonly in x–rays.

### Barium Sulfate
### BaSO4

In mineral form it is known as barium sulfate. Spiritually, the element of barium brings an energy of transparency, allowing us to see though the masks we wear and allows truth to come to light. Truth, honesty, and justice are the virtues of this element.

### Cayce Uses

In the life readings, Barium was referred to as an enema, or ingestible liquid that allows doctors to easily see and diagnose complications in the digestive track.

### Sample Barium Readings
### 1196-14 Reports
### G.I. Series made for [1196]

Fluoroscopic examination—Esophagus was observed, throughout its entire length, which appeared to be normal. Barium on entering the stomach rapidly passed to pyloric area.

## 257-217 Reports

Barium enema examination at that time was said to have revealed no other significant findings.

# *Beryllium*
## Be
## Atomic Number 4

### History

Beryllium is a rare alkaline earth metal originating from the mineral beryl, the same family of minerals as emerald and aquamarine. French chemist Louis–Nicolas Vauquelin discovered beryllium in 1798 while investigating the structures of emerald and beryl, once thought to be two totally different minerals.

Beryllium also led to the discovery of the neutron in 1932 after James Chadwick, the English physicist and Nobel Prize winner, discovered that bombarding beryllium with alpha particles caused a nuclear reaction that created neutrons.

### Beryllium Aluminum Silicate
### $Be_3Al_2(SiO_3)_6$

In mineral form, beryl is found in elongated shards with many different colors including green, blue, and pink. It is powerful stone of transformation and assists us in healing both physical ailments and situations. Several varieties, including emerald, aquamarine, and morganite, will be explored later in the book.

### Cayce Uses

Life readings were requested by executives of the Beryllium Corporation and much of Cayce's work in this area dealt with the profitability of the business. Amazingly, Cayce was able to deliver extremely detailed and complex information about the mining and alloying, or mixing, of metals—things normally only known by seasoned metallurgists.

### Sample Beryl Readings
### 1734-1

(Q) Will it be possible to work pure Beryllium?
(A) To make for commercial usage would be better to work same with its affinities, both above and below in the scale of metals, and not in its pure form.

### 1734-2

(Q) Regarding Beryllium, what metal below Beryllium in the scale of metals has most affinity for Beryllium?
(A) Tin.

## *Bismuth*
### Bi
### Atomic Number 83

### History

Bismuth was first described in 1450 by Basilius Valentinus, a German Monk, who called it wismut. It was constantly being confused with lead and tin but was not identified as an element until 1659 by Johann Glauber, and it was not separated from its ore until 1753 by Claud Geoffroy.

Bismuth is an ingredient in Pepto-Bismol, commonly used today to treat stomach disorders.

In the early twentieth century, infant mortality was very high due to an illness called "cholera infantum." A doctor from New York developed a formula he called Mixture Cholera Infantum made from Bismuth, zinc, and wintergreen that drastically improved the symptoms, and infant deaths began to decline. The mixture was colored pink, and after becoming mass-produced, was renamed Pepto-Bismol in 1919.

Native bismuth crystals are rare. It can be found more often as a nugget with other minerals included in the specimen. They can occasionally be found in Germany and Bolivia. Other minerals with Bismuth in them include: Bismuthinite, Pucherite, Walpurgite, and Emplectite.

Energetically, bismuth is a grounding element that soothes the nervous system and provides both physical and psychic protection. When the mineral specimen is placed on the stomach, it can provide the same relief to the digestion as Pepto-Bismol while healing ulcers and repairing tissue damage from stomach stress at a cellular level.

One of my clients suffered from a pre-ulcer condition caused by stress. The nervousness led to an acidic buildup, and he was warned to relax or suffer the consequences. Bismuth and its related minerals are good antidotes to such conditions if they can be located. The mineral can actually mend and heal the tears and bring the body back into a state of complete perfection when combined with meditating and allowing the body to rest.

### Cayce Uses

Appearing 769 times in 569 readings, Milk of Bismuth was continually recommended for any ailment of the stomach or digestive system. Cayce's recommendations of the mixture began in 1930, only a decade after it was first made available. It was prescribed for all sorts of illness, including alkalinity, acidity, toxemia, arthritis, tumors, stomach spasms, diarrhea, constipation, epilepsy, and ulcers.

### Sample Bismuth Readings
### 900-468

The Bismuth furnishes that as a coating for the whole intestinal system, and *prevents* regurgitation . . .

### 556-12

(Q) Should the Bismuth be combined with the Pepsin and taken?
(A) It's prepared in that way and manner. Bismuth-Pepsin, or Pepsinized (Peptonized) Bismuth.

## *Brass*
### Copper and Zinc Alloy

### History

Brass is an alloy, or mixture, of Copper and Zinc that was discovered after the Bronze Age, probably because Zinc is not easy to refine.

Brass is rarely found naturally except in Siberia, Russia, and because of that, it may one day be classified as a mineral—as long as it can be found in some quantity and is different from other copper and zinc mixtures.

Brass links us with our past. It can greatly enhance the recall of many past lives and the frequency can assist you with healing those lives or dealing with unfinished business.

### Cayce Uses

Cayce primarily referenced brass as it related to the advancements of several early civilizations including Atlantis and Egypt and during biblical times. He also made several mentions of "sounding brass," which could be referring to Corinthians in the Bible.

### Sample Brass Readings
### 364-12

With these developments came then the gradual injections of the use of elements from without for protection, as implements with which to protect themselves, which began with the use of *fitting* stone, iron, brass, copper, and those elements known in the present, as instruments of warfare, or of building, or of preservation of the various emoluments of individuals.

### 378-16

At the completion of that called Gizeh, there was the mounting of that which completed the top, composed of a combination or fluxes of brass, copper, gold, that was to be sounded when all the initiates were gathered about the altar or the pyramid.

### 364-13

Iron, brass, and copper were also employed even before the first upheavals.

  The early Atlanteans were peaceful and so made rapid

advances in the application of natural laws.

### 254-50
... an *idea* may be beautiful, may be wonderful, but without the background of an *ideal* becomes as but sounding brass, or as the gourd without water.

### Biblical References

Brass is mentioned several times in the Bible; however, in the New International Version, it is replaced with the word copper. In the time of the King James translation, brass was a popular material; in biblical times, however, copper would most likely have been the metal used, because brass was not around then.

> "Though I speak with the tongues of men and of angels, and have not charity, I am become as sounding brass, or a tinkling cymbal." Corinthians I 13:1

> "And he made the horns thereof on the four corners of it; the horns thereof were of the same: and he overlaid it with brass. And he made all the vessels of the alter, the pots, and the shovels, and the basins, and the fleshhooks, and the firepans: all the vessels thereof made he of brass." Exodus 38:2-3

> "And the pins of the tabernacle, and of the court round about, were of brass." Exodus 38:20

## *Bronze*
### Copper and Tin Alloy

### History

The Bronze Age began around 3600 B.C. after someone accidentally discovered that if you mix copper with tin, a new stronger material emerges that makes sharper tools and weapons than pure copper alone. This was a huge leap forward in the development of mankind. The chronology of the Bronze Age varies in different parts of the world. In any culture, the discovery of bronze occurred after the discovery of copper and preceded the discovery of iron which would provide even further enhancements to mankind. It is a time categorized by the fact that tools and weapons were made of bronze and can give amazing clues as to the developmental timelines of various cultures around the world.

Prior to discoveries in the 1960s, the Bronze Age was thought to have begun in the Middle East until new findings in Ban Chiang, Thailand, showed bronze technology dating back to as early as 4500 B.C.

Spiritually, bronze will connect you with other past lives where you experienced those energies. You can lay bronze on the body to provide a high frequency metal that will strengthen the aura while clearing it of blockages that may be tough to get through to with other stones and elements. It acts as a spiritual coat of armor and will protect the entire energy field from drains and psychic attack.

### Cayce Uses

Cayce's referrals to bronze dealt with the decorative or ornamental uses of the metal.

### Sample Bronze Readings
### 538-72

Above this—not too large and yet not in an oval, though the figures in the background shaded together would indicate an oval—the central figure, or the larger, would be the goddess Isis, *with* Horus upon the lap; this indicating especially the body of the goddess with the headdress, to be sure, of Taurus, or in that form, with the figure of the sun as the symbol in or between the horns of same. All of this would be in bronze color, save the center sun symbol which would be white. Indicate the special significance to Horus in the heart, or the manner of the entity's development towards children, motherhood, and the activities.

Put in the center the hand holding a torch. The hand would be in flesh color, the torch in bronze, the light in white and red, or red flame with white shadow above same; indicating the giving out to others.

## Biblical References
Bronze is referred to as brass in the King James version of the Bible, yet in the New International Version, that word is sometimes replaced with bronze because the Bronze Age came before brass was discovered.

# *Cadmium*
## Cd
## Atomic Number 48

### History
Cadmium is a rare metal that is only obtained as a byproduct of refining copper, lead, and zinc. Cadmium is used in electroplating, photography, engraving, transistors, and yellow oil–based paint. It was discovered accidentally in 1817 by chemist Friedrich Strohmeyer when he noticed a peculiar yellow coloring in some zinc ore he was analyzing; he realized it was a new element. Cadmium gets its name from the Greek word *kadmeira*, which is "calamine," a name referring to a skin lotion.

Cadmium is a very scarce element that cannot be found as a mineral in nature. It is found in a mineral called Otavite ($CdCO_3$), and Greenockite (CdS), which is the only real ore of cadmium. Cadmium usually comes from the processing of lead and zinc ore because it is found as a trace element within them.

### Cayce Uses
The cadmium in the readings is an ingredient in an oil Cayce prescribed for a three–year–old girl who fell and suffered a head injury.

### Sample Cadmium Readings
### 3375-1 Reports
[Q] What is the calamus (or cadmus, as pronounced in the reading) oil? Where may it be obtained? . . .
  Is it a solution of cadmium salts?
[Note by Gladys Davis: I find this definition under the

word cadmium: "calamine, a bluish white metal resembling zinc in its general properties. In its physiological action it is escharotic and astringent; internally, in large doses, it produces emesia and violent gastritis. Calmium iodide, used as an ointment, 1 to 8 of lard—calmium salicylate, white needles, soluble in water and alcohol—is said to be a more antiseptic activity than other cadmium salts—cadmium sulphate, an astringent in gonorrhea and in corneal opacities; used as a lotion in strength of H gr. or 4 to 1 ozs. of water, or as an ointment in 1:40 of fresh lard.]

### 3375-2

[A] While the cadmium indicated would be the salts mixed with lard, we will change these; so these may be the administrations!

## *Calcium*
### Ca
### Atomic Number 20

### History

Sir Humphrey Davy discovered calcium, the fifth most abundant element, in 1808. Several minerals include calcium including limestone, gypsum, calcite, and marble. The walls of caverns and caves are all made from calcium deposits. It is the building block of our bones and will help you stand strong in any situation. Obviously, minerals with calcium help prevent osteoporosis and bone disorders.

### Apatite
### $Ca_5(PO_4)_3(F,OH,Cl)$

Apatite, as the name suggests, is used to curb the appetite. There are many varieties and colors ranging from blue to green. It can help you lose weight, or if that is not what is needed, it can help you feel okay with the way things are going for you. It brings a sense of gratitude and inner peace.

## Gypsum/Selenite
## CaSO4*2H2O

Selenite, as I like to call it, is one of the most powerful stones of the New Age. It brings light into the energetic bodies and instantly clears all chakras. It is one of the few stones that does not ever need to be cleansed. It can be used to cleanse other stones as well. There are some great wands from Morocco that are very powerful healing tools. Wands can be used to direct energy and act as an extension of your energy and intent.

## Limestone

Limestone makes up so much of our planet and is an important geological part of the earth. It is like the bones of the planet that carry the weight of us all and hold everything together. So many tremendous mineral deposits are found among limestone. It is as if the bones hold the entire being of the planet in place so the gems can exist peacefully, each gem representing an organ of the body—so precious and rare and vital to the whole, yet it could not exist without the structural support of limestone. Limestone is excellent in healing any bone ailments from cancers to bone density issues, such as osteoporosis, to scoliosis. It can also be used to bring balance to areas where too much calcium has built up causing painful over-calcified joints by assisting the excess to spread more evenly around the body.

### Limestone Readings

Limestone is mentioned in the readings primarily in regards to the location of oil deposits:

### 4416-1

(Q) Would the well be drilled with Standard or Rotary tools?
(A) Should be begun with Rotary tools; through the second and third with Standard. The Hartselle Limestone will be too hard to drill with Rotary.

There are also references to the bone-building properties of limestone, and Cayce confirms it can be used to build teeth, gums, and soft tissue:

### 3211-2

(Q) ... could limestone in solution be added to this combination? And would it be beneficial as a cleanser of the
teeth? Would it be good as a commercial dentifrice in this
form?
(A) Not adding to the abilities of a cleansing agent, but
adding to the soft tissue for a builder-upper, as might be
called, to the gums and soft tissue of mouth and throat, it
would be well.

### Chalk

Although the days of blackboards and chalk are well over in the
schools across the country, it is too bad. Chalk is a wonderful calcium
based substance that held a nurturing energy that is now missing in
most schools with the advent of the dry erase board and the chemical
markers. Chalk is a wonderful tool for little children to use to draw with
on sidewalks. It allows them to tap into their soul roots in other lifetimes and remember the days of cliff drawings and hieroglyphics. As
they access these dormant memories of the soul, hidden talents are
released and it becomes easier for them to wake up and realize soul
purpose, so they may complete it in this lifetime. Many special children
are being born now to come in and assist us with vibrational and frequency shifts on the planet. The sooner these special earth angels wake
up and remember their missions, the better off we will all be. Chalk
provides the creative outlet and the nurturing energy so that children
feel safe and secure while bringing in this information.

### Chalk Readings

Chalk was frequently prescribed by Cayce to ease stomach discom-
forts and itching:

### 1005-6

(Q) Any local application for the itching?
(A) There may be added for that where the irritation be-

comes severe, those of Magnesia, Chalk and Tolu. This would be rubbed on. The tolu is, of course, that as is powdered. (Q) To be put on as a powder or an ointment? (A) As powder.

### 187-2

Chalk, Magnesia, or Petrolagar, may be well to give the body in small quantities, keeping the system, or the stomach, sweet with small doses of any of those conditions that bring the normal digestion in system . . . Each would tend to reduce also the acid in the system.

### Calcite
### CaCO3

Although Cayce did not mention calcite by name in the readings, I believe it is one of the most important minerals on the planet at this time. It is an excellent source by which we may tap into the element of calcium and all the healing properties it contains. Calcite comes in many colors and varieties including red, blue, green, and yellow. All of these have similar healing properties, depending on which one you are attracted to. Calcite is a soothing, protective stone that is excellent to calm the nerves and ease problems with digestion, including everything from stomachaches to alleviation of food poisoning symptoms.

One of the most important calcite deposits to date comes from the mine in Elmwood, Tennessee, which was recently closed. Usually calcite comes in cube-like formations, yet the Tennessee calcite is quite different structurally. It is found in huge golden-yellow crystals. The stones form this mine are particularly special, although there are also some very sweet pieces of calcite from China. The energy of the two are totally different, yet both bring something very important to the planet at this time.

Golden calcite is currently carrying the frequency of the yellow ray, meaning it is vibrating at the same speed as the color yellow. This is the color that activates your solar plexus chakra, and because of that it is a stone that allows you to stand tall in your power, be courageous, and hold your ground.

The sister to the amethyst called citrine was previously holding the yellow ray, but as planetary vibrations are shifting at an ever-increasing rate, the golden calcite has moved in to take its place. It is a much more peaceful energy than the citrine. Using the stone makes you feel like you are being held and comforted with a warm blanket wrapped around you. It is very nurturing and makes you feel as though everything will be okay, no matter how chaotic things may appear in the world. It is one of the most important stones of the Age of Aquarius, and I believe it will continue to be so for the next 100 years.

### Cayce Uses

It should be no surprise that there are over 850 references to calcium in 590 documents. Calcium is such an important building block for our body and Cayce clearly recognized that by offering several solutions for bringing more calcium into the body through diet and supplements. Calcium also helps circulation.

### Sample Calcium Readings
### 2470-2

(Q) Should I begin the calcium shots again?

(A) We would preferably take calcium in a more soluble form, or that as may be better assimilated; such as in Calcios, and in calcium-producing foods—such as turnips, turnip greens, and those of that nature, as well as in the masticating of the small bony pieces especially of chicken—chicken neck, feet and the like. And spread lightly a whole wheat cracker with Calcios (as you would butter) and take every other day.

(Q) What causes the cold spot in left side of back, and what should be done to correct it?

(A) Poor circulation. Stimulate better circulation through reducing the infectious forces. This may be done in the manner indicated, and aided with the proper amount, or better balance, of calcium.

# *Carbon*
## C
### Atomic Number 6

### History
Carbon is the giver of life. In the molecules of almost all plants and animals, there is one common factor that links us all—carbon. It is the element that allows complex strings of atoms to be connected and is the primary component of our DNA, which is a complex carbon molecule.

### Charcoal
Diamond is the crystalline form of carbon and is one of the most beloved members of the mineral kingdom, which we will look at later in the book. Coal is a non-crystaline form of carbon. All forms of carbon have the potential to realign and heal our DNA, as well as assist in the activation of dormant DNA. There is a theory that humans have many strands of DNA lying dormant at the present time that we used to have connected and that by reactivating these strands, enlightenment can be achieved. Any form of carbon will work in assisting this process. You may not be able to go out and purchase several natural diamonds for use in healing, but coal can work the same at a fraction of the cost. And if the DNA is to be healed and reactivated in stages, coal can be used for the initial awakening. The other forms act as stepping stones up the DNA chain until all are activated and functioning.

### Charcoal Readings
Charcoal is a popular natural remedy for all kinds of stomach ailments.

Cayce himself had over two hundred readings during his lifetime and charcoal was recommended for him to use in the elimination of toxins in his system:

### 294-64
Applying then those vibrations, as has been given, in the way and manner as has been given, with those properties to produce the normal eliminations through the intesti-

nal tract, and giving the digestive system that strength to produce that necessary equilibrium for the eliminations to be carried in their normal manner from the system. Keep intestinal tract open, adding charcoal—bismuth— and those properties to the system that will cause the system to function more normal, see?

## 550-1

Toxins produce taxation to the nervous system. The nervous system produces a taxation to the brain and sympathetic system. Hence we have that tired, dull, achey feeling, and the tendency to feel every bodily ailment that may come to the body, see? We have a complete cycle in these physical conditions.

Now, to *overcome* these would be to take properties in the system that will produce nearer the correct assimilations. These we will find under present existing conditions in that of one Charcoal Tablet each day.

### Graphite

Graphite, the material used to make pencils, is also a form of carbon. Synthetic diamonds are made of heated graphite, and although they are not considered as beautiful as naturally occurring diamonds, they are used in industry because they are just as hard as the real thing. These specimens can be used as the next step from the coal up the ladder of DNA activation. Graphite is the elemental form of carbon so it is a purer form of the element. The potential for using carbon in healing is limitless, if you consider that it is what makes up life, the goal in healing is to strengthen the life force and there is no better substance to use than carbon.

### Graphite Readings

There is only one reading with a reference to graphite. Cayce was at a private home where one of the people there mentioned it in a psychic reading he was giving to someone about levitating:

### 195-68 Reports

Regarding the graphite, this is what I was trying to show her; should the graphite be taken from the body entirely, then the body would be levitated, as she saw herself and myself rising to the ceiling. As time goes on, and this mind studies more, it may be given to [195] how to dispense with this danger. That is, the problem is, to take out just sufficient graphite as to cause the vacuum to allow the sun's rays to lift a weight without lifting the human being likewise.

### Carbon Steel

Cayce absolutely understood the importance of carbon in healing, especially one variety, carbon steel. This was used as an immune system builder and can fight off the common cold and build a wall of protection around you and your family. Carbon steel is an extremely important part of the Edgar Cayce readings and was mentioned 41 times. Based on the following reading and many testimonials of this remedy, carbon steel is sold in the Baar natural products catalog.

Carbon is also one of the main components of the wet cell battery, which Cayce recommends to everyone as a remedy for: "any condition relating to the vibratory forces in physical body, especially that of first stages of rheumatism, catarrh, or any condition that affects the system regarding the eliminations for the body." (1800-5)

### Carbon Steel Readings
### 1842-1

Do not take this as being something of superstition, or as something that would be a good luck charm—but if the entity will wear about its person, or in its pocket, a metal that is carbon steel—preferably in the groin pocket—it will prevent, it will ionize the body—from its very vibrations— to resist cold, congestion, and those inclinations for disturbance with the mucous membranes of the throat and nasal passages.

This is a needed element, then, about the body.

### 1842-1 Reports

I began with this product on 12-27-72, and will keep this carbon steel around my neck until I die.

Harsh words aren't they? Results—This part amazes me to this day. I put this piece of steel around my neck the day I received it. To my surprise, "within three hours," yes, three hours, I noticed a big, big change within my body. My cold actually began to break up. I couldn't believe what had happened. To this day, I have been out in all kinds of weather while I am at work and others have began to get sniffles, and I have yet to sneeze. I have not taken anything, no cold tablets or anything, only the steel around my neck. The cold disappeared and has not returned, and I hope it never will. Ratings—"Excellent."

### 1800-5

This we find would be well that everyone use such appliance, for the system would be improved in every condition that relates to the body being kept in attunement, as it were; for the forces as are exerted are such that the body responds to those conditions as are made by such an appliance, when constructed in the way and manner as given. Thus: Using two pieces carbon steel (plain, see?).

### Steel

Steel is mentioned in the readings 566 times—many of these readings deal with the stock market.

### Steel Readings
### 3422-1

As we find, from these vibrations, there are those effects from metallic substance that, because of certain elements in the blood supply, produce a very disagreeable and a very aggravating rash—wherever portions of the body become damp; forming into a running sore, or weeping eczema. The better manner to cope with the condition, as we find, is to change the environs, the surroundings. We would find better conditions if the activities were entirely in steel, or in other forms of metal than chromium or aluminum.

### 900-280

(Q) What, if anything, does this portend as to steel stock price?

(A) This, as has been given, that with the declaring of dividends there will become that advance as is seen for same, when much of same will be found in the hands of those who are gradually taking hold of same under the existent conditions.

## *Chromium*
### Cr
### Atomic Number 24

### History

Discovered by French chemist Louis–Nicolas Vauquein in 1797, chromium gets its name from the Greek word *chromos* meaning "color" because it can often produce green, red and yellow colors. Rubies get their red color and emeralds get their green color from the trace amounts of chromium found within them.

Chromium provides an etheric shield for the subtle energy bodies, preventing any unwanted energies from passing through. This shield gives off a very high frequency that can act as a transmitter for sounds from higher dimensions of consciousness to pass through and deliver intuitive messages to the user, and chromium can be used to develop and enhance the gift of clairaudience.

Besides emerald and ruby, several other minerals have traces of chromium in them including alexandrite, chromite, the ore of chromium, and uvarovite.

### Stichtite
### Mg6Cr2CO3(OH)164H2O

Stichtite is another chromium–based mineral from Tasmania. It is a very unusual thin, light purple metallic-like stone with ties to the seven sister planets of the Pleiades. Stichtite allows us to connect with the energy of the Pleiades and the inhabitants of those planets who are coming in to assist us with various aspects of earth changes. It is an extremely high frequency stone that allows us to hear and access not only the advice and counsel from our brothers in space, but our own higher mind.

### Cayce Uses

Cayce never recommended the use of chromium, and in fact, told someone to avoid those vibrations. Like many readings, that suggestion is meant for the particular individual who received the reading. These days, you will find chromium picolinate tablets at all of the health food stores as a natural weight loss solution. Chromium helps the body burn stored fat and increases metabolism. The question about any possible long term side effects from this remains to be seen.

### Sample Chromium Readings
### 3422-1

(Q) Please suggest an occupation that would be better.
(A) As indicated, work in any other type of metal—just so it is not chromium or aluminum. Steel would be better than tin or such combinations where there are the filings of metals, for the body should refrain from activity with these.

## *Copper*
### Cu
### Atomic Number 29

### History

Copper got its name from the Latin word *cuprum*, meaning "from Cyprus." Despite its common uses in electrical wiring, copper is actually a rather rare element comprising only .007 percent of the earth's crust.

Copper has been around since the dawn of civilization, evidenced by the discovery of copper jewelry found in Iraq from 9000 B.C. It is considered humanity's first metal showing up in ancient Sumeria and Egypt. The Egyptians were extremely skilled in working with copper, making everything from tools, cookware, and adornments such as headdresses and crowns. Copper plates were placed under the heads of the dead to assist them in the transition into the afterlife.

Because it is an excellent transmitter of electricity, these properties can be used on the physical body to balance out electrical flow and energy within the body and bring balance. It can also bring mental balance and clarity and create the needed energy to shift situations.

Arthritic conditions and circulation challenges can be addressed with copper. Lately the magnetic copper bracelets are popular. Using two magnets, one at each end of a band of copper, the bracelet can be worn and pain from arthritis may be lessened. Copper also helps the blood flow to the entire body, including, of course, the brain, so copper can also be used to enhance learning or memory. It can be used to increase circulation of the blood, increasing the flow of oxygen to various parts of the body.

I have used copper on clients suffering from crippling cases of gout and arthritis with amazing results. The copper tends to reduce swelling and increase mobility to stiff joints quickly.

### Cayce Uses

Mentioned 1205 times in over 600 readings, copper is used with other elements to produce both the wet cell battery and the radio-active device. Copper plates and nickel plates are recommended extensively because: "Copper and nickel are specified for the contacts because the one (copper) is strongly positive and the nickel is negative." (1800-34 Reports)

In the readings, copper is used to treat: cerebral palsy, epilepsy, dermatitis, birth injuries, and anemia.

### Sample Copper Readings
### 4491-1

(Q) Should both plates be of copper, and what size?

(A) One of copper, one of nickel, very thin, just sufficient size that the vibrations may be received by the body, so that they will fasten around wrist and around ankle, left side and right side.

## *Cobalt*
### Co
### Atomic Number 27

### History

Cobalt is a rare bluish–white metal found in igneous, or volcanic, rock. Discovered by Georg Brandt in 1737, it was previously mistaken with copper. Cobalt blue, used to color everything from glassware to cosmetics, is made from aluminum oxide mixed with cobalt [(Co(AlO2)2]. Cobalt is also an essential trace element in our diet because it is a natural source of vitamin B12.

### Roselite
### $Ca_2(CoMg)(AsO_4)_2 \cdot 2H_2O$

Roselite is a rare pink–colored stone form Germany that has ancient links to the Knights Templar and the Rosy Cross. It will also connect you with the pure energy of love represented by the rose.

### Cayce Uses

Cayce recognized the needed trace elements in the diet and recommended hundreds of people take a supplement called Calcios that contained cobalt, calcium, and other mineral elements. Because color therapy was also an important part of the readings, cobalt blue light was recommended to assist and calm the nervous system.

### Sample Cobalt Readings
### 1564-1
### CALCIOS

A diet supplement of young bone, marrow, protein, and essential minerals in colloidal form for better assimilation; calcium, cobalt, iron, magnesium, manganese, phosphorus, potassium, sodium, sulphur, and zinc. These elements are in trace amounts and with naturally occurring associated factors such as found in young bone and marrow.

### 302-9

*Coordination* of eliminations, and more of the vitality in assimilations in the system are needed. Such vital energy may be aided—not without the use of those as have been given—but by *varying* the character of the lights for the body. The ultra-violet changed to the Infra Red, as well as the green and blue. Cobalt blue, and nile green.

# *Gold*
## Au
## Atomic Number 79

### History

Gold is the most precious and stunning of all elements. It has been a treasured part of society since ancient times. The chemical symbol comes from the Latin word aurum, which means *"shining dawn,"* and the name gold is derived from the Sanskrit word for gold, *jval.*

Gold is a masculine metal. It is the yang—the forceful aggressive energy of conquerors and rulers and has been used by these types of people for ages. Wearing gold will enable you to become more aggressive in your life and to go and get what you want. The color gold is very powerful in healing. It creates a spiritual wall of protection around those who use it that cannot be penetrated. In hypnosis and guided imagery work, I always have the client imagine the golden ball of protective light around them. It serves as a psychic shield so that no ill can come to the person on their journey.

### Aqua Aura

Aqua aura is a relatively new stone to hit the market. It is a man-made infusion of eighteen carat gold into quartz, yielding a beautiful turquoise–aqua colored stone. Aqua aura allows the user to tap into the powerful healing forces of gold without having to pay the high price for nuggets or gold-plated jewelry. Aqua aura has fast become one of my favorite stones. It brings feelings of joy, peace, and inner tranquility to the user and can be used to strengthen the immune system.

### Cayce Uses

Gold is listed in the readings 4134 times in 1667 documents. Gold Chloride solution was a prominent prescription as part of the Wet Cell Battery regimen. Main uses for it were: (1) treatment of multiple sclerosis, (2) burns or skin ailments, (3) aid in pregnancy, gold was recommended internally "to aid conception, to produce greater ovulation," and (4) any disturbance of the glandular or nervous system.

### Sample Gold Readings
### 1134-1

Begin, then, with the use of the low form of electrical vibration carrying the elements that are in their very nature reactory to the glandular forces of the body; that is, Gold—in a Chloride state, and Silver—in a Nitrate state.

### 852-12

(Q) Is there any particular stone or stones I should wear?
(A) Gold in the forms of circles or of many bangles, and the like, are greater to the entity than stones; save diamonds.

### 5125-1

For the entity was among those who had come from portions of Alabama and settled in what is now Arkansas (or Ar-Kansas as then called); and the entity was among those who panned for gold and found diamonds.

### Biblical References

"And he made the vessels which were upon the table, his dishes, and his spoons, and his bowls, and his covers to cover withal, of pure gold. And he made the candlestick of pure gold . . . " Exodus: 38:16-17

"My fruit is better than gold, yea, than fine gold; and my revenue than choice silver." Proverbs 8:19

# *Hydrogen*
## H
### Atomic Number 1

### History

Hydrogen is the most abundant element in the universe with the simplest atomic structure. Most of the earth's hydrogen is found in the oceans, rivers, and streams.

### Water
### $H_2O$

Water is considered to be one of the four elements of nature along with air, fire, and earth. It is the most powerful force on the planet, and the ocean accounts for most of the life on earth. In healing, the element of water is powerful for dealing with emotions, particularly with broken hearts. Water soothes and relieves the heartache, eases the pain, and washes it away, leaving a peaceful tranquility in its place, because water carries the frequency of the blue ray which is restful and relaxing to the nervous system. Water has a profound impact on you physically, as well, since it is the primary component of the human body. If you are ever feeling unwell, water can often be a key to the restoration of health. These days, most people are not drinking enough water and suffer from various states of dehydration. Water is essential if you want to feel rested, refreshed, and balanced.

### Water Readings
### 1861-4

Do not confuse rote, or mental growth, with spiritual import. It is true that the combination of $H_2O$ constantly produces water. It is true that the bow upon the string at a certain tone constantly produces C, or another note, to which the attunement is made to a first cause—as the $H_2O$ is to a first cause. But it is not *always* water that is wanted with hydrogen and oxygen. Neither is it always C that is desired upon the tune or tone of the instruments.

## Ice
## H20

Believe it or not, ice is actually considered the mineral form of hydrogen known to chemists as hydrogen oxide. Ice allows things of the past to stay with us to be used in the future. Ice not only reduces swelling and fever, it can also reduce feelings of being overwhelmed or the negative impact of bad news. Ice energetically puts a distance between you and your worries or concerns by cooling off the worry and calming hot tempers. Ice facilitates change ending old energetic patterns, yet keeps the knowledge and learning preserved for future use. In situations that were not positive, ice allows them to pass while keeping the lesson fresh in your mind.

### Ice Readings

Among other things, Cayce suggested ice be used to prepare and cleanse the radioactive device before use, and to reduce nausea.

### 1800-14

(Q) Are these applicators in good working order?
(A) When cleansed, yes. That is, the anodes, see? And when in ice, see, or on ice, and these should be on ice at least, or ice around same, for ten to fifteen minutes before attachment to body, see?

### 826-7

(Q) Is manufactured ice preferable to ice made in an electric refrigerator, for the Radio-Active Appliance?
(A) Either will do. The manufactured ice is *preferable* because it carries that which will make for more effectiveness. The preferable manner, of course, would be to use dry ice; but any of it is all right just so it makes activities for the system.

### 325-69

(Q) Can anything be done to relieve the severe nausea after taking the sedative?

(A) Ice upon the esophagus, or ice pack, with a hot pack upon the plexus at the cardiac portion of the stomach.

(Q) Do you mean ice pack at the same time using a hot pack?

(A) This would be better. Or if not ice, it may be a wet cold cloth over the cardiac or the throat, or vice versa.

### Cayce Uses for Hydrogen

The source spoke about hydrogen often when explaining the forces of the universe, or the natural element of water.

### Sample Hydrogen Readings
### 900-370

(Q) I was told that Death is separation just as death for a drop would be separation of its elements into hydrogen and oxygen.

(A) Correct. Each force as manifested in the various stages, or states, being as that illustration of the various stages a life may manifest in its varied forms, either before combined in hydrogen and oxygen becoming water.

### 4031-1

(Q) Is all the hydrogen sulfide damage out of my system by now?

(A) Refractions might be expected, but the massages and the increasing of the eliminations through alimentary canal should soon purify system and allow for normal reactions.

# *Iron*
## Fe
## Atomic Number 26

### History

Iron has played a major role in civilization since the beginning of recorded history. The Iron Age, which began around 1100 B.C., was a major advance in human history. As the most common of all metals, iron affects all of our lives on a daily basis.

### Iron-Nickel

Iron is rarely seen on the earth's surface naturally. When it is found, it is usually the result of meteoric activity. All occurrences of iron on the earth surface are actually alloys of iron and nickel. The true origin of these deposits is a mystery. It is speculated that another planet broke apart and continues to shower earth with iron–nickel deposits because our own planet has these two elements at its core.

These specimens allow you to connect with universal energy and life forms on other planets, should you choose to do so. If you happen to acquire a piece, I recommend you store it in a way that it can be protected from humidity because iron is prone to rust.

### Iron Pyrite
### FeS2

Iron Sulfide commonly mistaken for gold, pyrite is known as "fool's gold." Mined in several places, such as Colorado, Peru, Bolivia, Mexico, Romania, and Sweden, pyrite has a childlike energy that can activate and enhance the imagination. It is also a powerful psychic protector and will shield you from negativity, a trait of nearly all iron–based minerals.

Iron pyrite has been one of my favorite stones since childhood. It helps you stay in touch with your inner child, to the creative uncensored part of the self. It is a wonderful stone for artists or anyone in a creative field because it keeps all the possibilities open while providing enough grounding to get the work finished. Pyrite is also a protective stone for children. It wards off injuries and attacks and maintains the child's innocence.

### Hematite
### FeO3

An Iron Oxide, Hematite gets its name from the Greek word for blood, *"haima"* It is a powerful stone for repelling negativity and grounding. When used in healing it works to assist circulation through its magnetic properties, and when carried or worn as jewelry, it actually absorbs potentially hazardous vibrations and, if not cleansed regularly, will eventually crack.

Hematite is a very common and inexpensive stone. You have probably seen it as rings in stores. When worn, it is used to repel negativity. A great friend of mine bought a piece and gave it to her husband to hold right after he just lost his job. Within twenty-four hours, the stone had cracked in two. Nearly every place I go to lecture on gems and stones, I undoubtedly run into someone who has experienced the effects of a cracking piece of hematite.

### Cayce Uses

Cayce recommended iron-rich foods for people suffering with arthritis and reproductive organ weaknesses.

### Sample Iron Readings
### 255-3

(Q) Specify foods containing iron.

(A) These are they, as we find, as would respond with this body: Those of spinach, of cabbage, of turnips, of salsify, of radish, and of such natures. These add to the system. In the fruits, and for *this* body—well that pears be eaten. These add a characterization in iron that is well for any condition where there is improper fermentation. Some character of apples, those of lemons, those of oranges— *especially* those grown in certain localities. Those as found in Florida oranges carry more iron than those grown in California, while those of the southern states, or in the Rio Grande valley, carry more than those even in Florida.

## 1794-1

Use in the beginning not so much heavy foods, but rather the easily assimilated diet; soft or liquid or semi-liquid foods, but plenty of foods that carry iron. Plenty of figs, plenty of raisins, plenty of apricots, plenty of carrots; plenty of lettuce, red cabbage and the like.

### Biblical References

"A land wherein thou shalt eat bread without scarceness, thou shalt not lack any thing in it; a land whose stones are iron, and out of whose hills thou mayest dig brass."
Deuteronomy 8:9

# Lead
## Pb
## Atomic Number 82

### History

The ancient Romans used lead to make pipes for delivering water to the people in the cities because it was inexpensive, easy to form, and did not rust like iron. This could potentially account in part to the fall of that once great empire, because as we now know, lead is extremely toxic to humans.

Lead was used for making bullets in ancient weaponry, lead pencils were also used until they were replaced by graphite, a carbon-based substance. Lead was also used in paints because it created a protective coating that sealed in color and was resistant to erosion. It was used extensively in barns because it kept termites and other pests from eating the wood.

Lead in mineral form is called Minium ($Pb_3O_4$), or lead oxide. Lead minerals are used for grounding and keeping out unwanted low vibration energies from other dimensions. There are several other interesting lead-based minerals. A few of my favorites are mentioned here.

## Crocoite
## PbCrO4

Crocoite is a red lead ore, or lead chromate. It has extremely fragile bright red crystals protruding in all directions and is found in Tasmania, Australia. The red crystals ignite a fiery energy to those who are in its presence. Crocoite is an excellent stone for those who need more motivation because it literally starts a fire under the user. Like its other lead-based counterparts, it is a toxic substance and should be handled at a minimum. It is a great stone to leave in a space needing more brightness and energy.

## Galena
## PbS

Galena is a lead sulfide that occurs in cube-like formations on the side of calcite and other mineral deposits. It is a dark gray, shiny material that can be very grounding and centering to the user. It is a stone that should be used to ground energy in a space rather that on a person. Put it in a room with the intent that clarity and centeredness will prevail there. It can also bring states of clarity and feelings of peace by bringing calmness to the area. It is toxic, so should be handled rarely.

## Wulfenite
## PbMoO4

Wulfenite is a yellow lead ore found in Austria, Czechoslovakia, the Congo and Namibia, Africa, and Pennsylvania and Arizona, U.S.A. Like its red counterpart, Crocoite, Wulfenite also has crystals protruding in all directions, although these are more in flat sheet–like formations. Wulfenite brings the energy of excitement, courage, and steadfastness to situations requiring concentration and commitment. When placed in a room, it brings a sense of total balance with the infusion of energy and excitement needed to make a happy environment.

## Cayce Uses

Shortness of breath and elimination and heart problems are all credited to lead poisoning in the readings. Lead is also a critical component of the Wet Cell Battery.

### Sample Lead Readings
### 2201-1

There is seen, too, that this vein is at an angle, and that the lode divides into two distinct veins, a little distance from where the shaft would strike the lead, see? Or vein.

### 631-4

And use the Gold solution in a larger container, with a coil of the hollow lead such as used for soldering lead in the small lengths, see?

### Biblical References

"Thou didst blow with thy wind, the sea covered them: they sank as lead in the mighty waters." Exodus 15:10

"That they were graven with an iron pen and lead in the rock forever!" Job 19:24

## *Lithium*
### Li
### Atomic Number 3

### History

Lithium (Greek for "stone") is an extremely reactive lightweight metallic element used in the treatment of manic–depressive disorders. It was first discovered in 1817 by Swedish chemist Johan August Arfvedson and is used in the production of vitamin A. Arfvedson made the discovery by accident while performing a routine chemical analysis on some minerals in a Swedish mine.

### Lepidolite

In my book, *Gemstone Journeys*, I reported on the stone Lepidolite which is a lavender–colored mica used to alleviate insomnia and allow the user to experience fantastical out–of body journeys.

My brother is particularly fond of the Lepidolite stone and after I wrote the book, I discovered it is primarily Lithium based. The interesting thing about that is he is autistic and I have noticed since then that the stone can be used for all types of mental distress, including depression and anxiety.

### Lithium Quartz

One of the newer stones to become available is the Lithium Quartz, which has fragments of the element sprayed into quartz crystals. Currently, this material is being mined in Brazil, and similar to Lepidolite and other Lithium–based minerals, it provides the user with a sense of calm and peace. This should not be too surprising considering Lithium is used in the treatment of manic–depressive disorders. It creates balance and well-being and can enhance the release of endorphins into the system.

### Sugilite
### $KNa_2Li_3(Fe,Mn,Al)_2Si_{12}O_{30}$

Sugilite is another of the most important stones of the new age. It contains trace amounts of Lithium, and like Lithium Quartz and Lepidolite, it is also a lavender color. Sugilite is very high frequency and works to quickly open the third eye center giving you very profound psychic visions. It can be used by anyone wanting to develop the gift of clairvoyance. Because of the high spiritual energy of the stone, the visions it allows you to receive are of a very high spiritual nature and may occur in symbols rather than in the literal sense. Because of that, it is a stone prized by mystics and seers. The Lithium in the stone keeps the mental faculties of the visionary grounded in reality while the highest realms are looked into. It is particularly helpful in foreseeing the future of mankind and trends of humanity both to warn us about possible challenges and to give insights into opportunity.

### Cayce Uses

Lithium is used to aid circulation, elimination, kidney and liver support and to cleanse the blood supply.

## Sample Lithium Readings
### 2518-1

At all times drink plenty of water. Occasionally—say once a week—put a lithia tablet in a glass of water and drink it. This will stimulate better circulation and set up better drainage through the whole of the alimentary canal, especially as related to the hepatic circulation; that is, the circulation between the liver, the kidneys, and the flow through the alimentary areas of the body.

### 4244-1

(Q) What mineral elements are lacking in the system?
(A) Those of the proper building for the blood supply; iron, silicon, and as is given that of lithium.

## *Magnesium*
### Mg
### Atomic Number 12

### History

The seventh most abundant element on earth, magnesium, is prevalent in seawater and is one of the primary ingredients in Epsom Salts, discussed in the sodium section of the book. Milk of Magnesia is helpful in relieving stomach and digestive ailments, and assists in the absorption of calcium. In the plant kingdom, magnesium plays an important role in photosynthesis.

### Dolomite
### CaMg(CO3)2

Dolomite is a combination of magnesium, calcium, and oxygen. It is very soothing to the digestion, and heals ulcers and acidic stomach conditions. It will help make digestion regular and alleviates both diarrhea and constipation.

## Serpentine
## H4Mg3Si209

Serpentine is quickly becoming one of my preferred stones to use in healing. There are many different kinds, each are various shades of green. These stones are used to alleviate massive pain—arthritis, cancers, spinal conditions, or any extremely painful condition can be relieved with the stone. One client had severe back problems and used a piece of African serpentine known as Infinite. He taped the stone on his back and within a day the stone turned black and the pain was gone, never to return.

Serpentine is also used for raising kundalini, the serpent energy located at the base of the spine, discussed in Eastern texts.

## Talc
## Mg3Si4010(OH)2

Talc is a magnesium–based mineral that is mentioned extensively in the Cayce readings. Talc is a gentle mineral used as the model for Moh's Hardness Scale. This scale is how all gems are rated, and in the scale, talc is the softest mineral known.

It is soothing to the emotions and to the spirit. In powder, it physically protects the skin, and spiritually, it protects the aura and energetic bodies from psychic attack.

### Cayce Uses

Cayce recommends magnesia to be used internally to strengthen the body, as an aid during the final ten days before a woman gave birth, and to relieve tension in the gastrointestinal tract.

### Sample Magnesium Readings
### 4439-1

To give the strength then necessary, we would create within this body, those factors necessary to give elemental force to the body. They should have in their make up, magnesia, iron, sulphur, lithium, silicious [silicon], such as we would find in the spring, see.

**575-1**

And in the diet there should be more of the milk and Milk of Magnesia; these will aid in these latter days in making for the better flow to the body and in relieving the pressures respecting the irritations in the intestinal tract, making for general conditions of a better nature.

**294-73**

(Q) Would Milk of Magnesia help the acid condition?
(A) Milk of Magnesia would be very good.

## *Manganese*
**Mn**
**Atomic Number 25**

### History

Manganese is used as an alloy additive to harden steel. In healing it is a powerful stone for grounding and protection.

### Rhodonite
### (MnFe,Mg,Ca)5(SiO3)5

Rhodonite is a beautiful stone ranging from pale to dark pink. It is a profound healer of the emotional heart, helping you to mend past hurts and look toward the future. My favorite pieces come from Silverton, Colorado, home of the old silver mines. It brings a peaceful serene energy and calms the nervous system, which is something greatly needed today. It can gently alleviate pre–Parkinson's syndromes, Palsy's or any disorder of the nervous system where tremors are involved.

Recently several people have been stricken with various forms of nervous system disorders. Actor Dudley Moore died of Super–Nuclear Palsy; Roger Ebert has Bell's Palsy, which is essentially like a stroke causing partial paralysis of the facial muscles and a drooping of one side of the face; Michael J. Fox has long suffered from his very public battle with Parkinson's Disease. I believe all of these types of disorders are caused by the body's inability to handle the rapidly changing environmental vibrational frequency shifts.

Emotionally, it can represent the inflexibility of the body and unwillingness or fear of change.

Rhodonite can assist the body to gently release the fear of the unknown and allow you to gently adjust to changes in the world around you while raising your vibration.

### Rhodochrosite
### MnCO3

A close relative to the rhodonite, rhodochrosite, the ore of manganese, is also helpful in heart healing and assists the nervous system of the body. Rhodochrosite is a pink and white stone with beautiful agate-like bands running through it that usually form circular patterns. While the rhodonite can assist with the energetic and emotional parts of healing the nervous system, Rhodochrosite acts on the physical and cellular level to bring about the necessary changes to the body that will enable it to heal. It will show the body the proper form to take to expand the capacities of the nervous system and bring about physically healing changes.

### Manganese—Sugilite

One of the newer stones to hit the market is a combination of the purple third eye opening stone, manganese, with sugilite. This has been a favorite stone of mine that I have recommended to many people who have also reported wonderful results from its use. The Manganese ore allows the user to get a feeling of being profoundly grounded while the sugilite powerfully opens the third eye. By itself, manganese is a powerful grounding stone because it is a manganese with iron oxide. As mentioned earlier, iron is always a powerful stone for grounding and protection. The combination of manganese and sugilite allows you to stay focused on the physical plane while opening to high spiritual realms.

### Cayce Uses

In these readings Cayce demonstrated his amazing ability to understand metallurgy in trance. He knew how earth elements were formed and how they could best be used. Truly amazing.

## Sample Manganese Readings
### 1734-5

(Q) What is the proper flux to use in melting and alloying our metals and what is the proper method?
(A) With more manganese, this will make for a better gathering together of the atoms in the metal for a more perfect product, and will make for a better handling.

### 470-13

First, as has been indicated, in the separating of the ore from slags and impurities (which is necessary for its usage), for a great period an ordinary ore of one form or stage has passed through a state of preparation by the heating to such an intensity that, with the addition of the chlorate, the manganese and the carbon, it has brought forth—by its natural settlements, or natural sediments being removed—a state, or gained such a state (the ore) as to turn to metal.

## *Mercury*
### Hg
### Atomic Number 80

### History

Mercury is the only metal that is liquid at room temperature. Mercury is derived from the mineral cinnabar. The ore of cinnabar is heated up and when the vapor is condensed, it forms mercury. Most deposits of cinnabar come from Spain, where Mercury has been mined non–stop for the past 2000 years. As far back as 1500 B.C., mercury was discovered in Egyptian tombs.

### Cinnabar

The gem enthusiast can experience Mercury though its ore, cinnabar. This is one of the most powerful stones on the planet for abundance.

Unfinished, it is actually one of the most unattractive materials I have ever worked with. It looks like a white chalky–type substance with dark bright red streaks running through it. Samples can be found in Nevada. It is also found in China and can occur as beautiful deep red crystals. You have probably seen cinnabar necklaces and bracelets carved with ancient Asian symbols for prosperity. A well-known tool in the art of Feng Shui, cinnabar is used in ornaments and jewelry that are known to attract great wealth. Use this to bring more money into your life.

### Cinnabar Quartz
The newest mineral find in the cinnabar family is cinnabar quartz found in Arizona. The stone is being cut in extremely attractive cabochons for jewelry and has colorful bright red streaks running through multicolored stone. It is very attractive, and again, is a stone you should wear if you want to attract financial abundance to yourself.

### Cayce Uses
Mercury quartz lamps were recommended dozens of times by Cayce for a variety of disorders relating to the nervous system.

### Sample Mercury Reading
### 165-7
(Q) In Health Light Rooms will the best practice use carbon arc or mercury vapor lamps?
(A) These are two entirely different fields, and should ever be considered so. The mercury lamps are in one field, and are for those that offer the better elements for conditions of the nerve systems of the body; while the carbon will offer the greater developments for those that will aid deeper conditions and those that affect the structural portion of a body.

# *Nickel*
## Ni
## Atomic Number 28

### History

Nickel is found in the ore of a mineral called millerite, a combination of nickel and sulphur. It was originally isolated from its ore in 1751 by Swedish chemist Axel Fredrik Cronstedt. In the ancient world, Nickel was used to color glass and other things green. Nickel is extremely resistant to corrosion and has several uses. You're probably most familiar with the nickel coin, although these days, the coin is actually made up primarily of copper with a bit of nickel mixed in. It is also used commercially in batteries, stainless steel, and in the heating elements of toasters and ovens.

### Gaspeite
### (Ni,Mg,Fe)CO3

If you've traveled to Santa Fe lately or have been anywhere near Native American styled jewelry, you will see turquoise and coral in beautiful jewelry with a chartreuse, or apple–green colored stone. That stone is gaspeite. It is a nickel–based mineral found near nickel sulfide deposits. It is named after the area where it was originally located in the province of Quebec, Canada. Australia is another source for some of the best gaspeite.

When used with other stones such as the ones mentioned above, gaspeite brings an air of harmony and cooperation and can help you do the same. If you are in a situation where you need to be a team player, gaspeite brings the energy you need to contribute to the group without becoming too passive or too domineering. The light green color provides an energy of warmth and fellowship.

### Nickel Magnesite
### Ni2Mg

I ran across a rare specimen of pale lime green nickel magnesite from Australia I have not let out of my sight since. It is one of my new favorite stones—I'm sure by now you can tell I love them all! When I am traveling, I like to create a sacred space in a corner of whichever hotel or place I am staying in to bring a sense of centeredness to my travels. My nickel magnesite piece is always a part of that configuration. It seems to bring an energy of happiness and belonging, so no matter where you are, you feel you are part of any groups you encounter. It soothes the soul in times of upheaval and uncertainty and brings a feeling of security and sameness to unstable situations. Extensive travel can be quite unsettling at times; yet with this stone, you will feel at ease.

### Cayce Uses

As part of the Wet Cell Battery, nickel and copper plates were used on the device and recommended to people suffering from toxicity and other ailments. Cayce spent a lot of time explaining what we touched on briefly in the iron section—that iron and nickel occur together in nature, yet they are like polar opposites to each other so they can be used magnetically in the equipment.

### Sample Nickel Readings
### 465-1

Prepare, then, the wet cell battery, with two applicators that carry atomic forces to the system. Make the anodes or poles one of copper, the other of nickel; also the anodes or plates that are to be attached to the body should be of copper and of nickel or German silver—nickel preferable.

(Q) Is nickel applicator connected to nickel anode?
(A) The nickel pole and the nickel applicator are on the same leads, you see. The nickel that goes into solution is in the middle of the lead. Use nickel rather than lead or other elements, for we need the change in the vibration to create the proper vibration to the body itself through the low electrical vibrations created.

### 2366-7

Attach the nickel plate to the umbilical and lacteal duct plexus—that is, four fingers from the navel center to the right and two fingers up from that point.

### 819-2

(Q) Should both plates or anodes be of copper or nickel?
(A) One is the copper (the positive), the other is the nickel (the negative).

## *Platinum*
### Pt
### Atomic Number 78

### History

Platinum is a precious metal discovered by Charles Wood in England in 1741, and gets its name from the Spanish word "platina" or silver because of evidence it may have been used by pre–Columbian Indians.

Currently, most of the specimens are being mined from the Ural mountain range in Siberia. Although it is popular and is known as the most durable of the common metals used in jewelry, it is very rare to find such specimens as those now being mined from the Urals. This new deposit was discovered inside a crater–like structure, known as an alluvial deposit, which is extremely unusual for platinum.

I had the unique opportunity to meet with some of the people in charge of the mines in the Urals and got to hold a huge piece (by huge, I only mean about two inches long by an inch in diameter) in my hand valued at over $37,000US. It was quite a powerful stone, and I did not want to let it go! The platinum brings an energy that is bigger than life. It makes you feel grounded and cosmic at the same time. It is a metal of big dreams and aspirations, boosting self-confidence and the ability to see things through. Belief in self and belief that you can change the world are the energies of platinum. Because the metal is so tough, it also gives you the feeling that nothing can stop you from living your dreams; you are invincible and bigger than life. It is the kind of energy you had when you were a child, until the world got in your way and made you think dreaming big was foolish. Platinum can revive the childlike you to create a powerful future.

## Angel Aura

Angel Aura is a relatively new manmade stone derived from electro-plating platinum on to quartz, similar to the gold in aqua aura. Because platinum is often hard to find as a mineral sample, Angel Aura allows the user to tap into the powerful healing vibrations of this metal.

Platinum creates a vibrational state of transformation. It allows the user to transcend negativity, becoming uplifted to new heights and realms. It is excellent to use when undergoing a career or major life change where you are directed to go off into entirely new and previously unknown situations. Its high frequency raises the users vibration to meet any challenge and is flexible enough to allow the user to practically shift gears to fit whatever is needed at the time.

## Cayce Uses

For vibrational purposes, Cayce recommended someone wear it.

## Sample Platinum Readings
### 1620-2

In the material things—wear as an ornament, preferably a ring, the moonstone; and have the activities of all the influences of metals, especially the platinum, about thee. Their vibrations are in accord with that to keep thy animation in accord with the best thou may accomplish.

### 165-14

(Q) What is the name of the ore?
(A) Those in which it, the element sought, is next to—is platinum, or platinite—of gold, and arsenic.

### 440-3

(Q) What elements would be combined to use in place of crystal?
(A) Uranium, platinite—or platinum in its basic form, and gold (from which the arsenic is taken).

# *Potassium*
## K
### Atomic Number 19

### History

Potassium is a very reactive silver–white metal that, like its counter-parts Sodium and Lithium, is never found alone in nature. Like sodium, potassium is found most often in the oceans but is not as abundant as sodium because the plants use it for growth. It is another of the many elements first isolated from its ore in 1807 by Sir Humphrey Davy.

Potassium is used in fertilizers for plants and trees, which is where humans used to get much of their potassium intake.

### Charoite
### K(NaCa)11(Ba,Sr)Si18O46(OH,F)·nH2O

Charoite, an extremely complex mineral, is only found in one river bed along the Chary River in Russia. It is an extremely rare stone because this is the only place where this type mineral has ever been found. It is a light purple colored stone with swirls of white and dark blue. Spiritually, Charoite is another great stone for opening up psychically and facilitates the gifts of both clairvoyance and clairsentience, or the ability to feel things psychically.

You may find yourself drawn to this stone as a way to energetically connect to and heal past lives in Siberia. Certain people are inexplicably drawn to the stone, and what I have found is that often means that energetically the stone is assisting with healing karma from the place where the stone is from.

I happen to love charoite, so I would imagine I probably spent a time or two in the cold mountains of Siberia at some time in the past. While holding a piece one day, I found myself going within and staring at a snow packed trail along a mountain range I have never seen in this lifetime. I can only assume that the stone is helping me with some aspect of that particular past life.

### Cayce Uses

Mentioned over 1000 times, 905 of which refer to Potassium Bromide or Iodide. One is a sedative and the other a gland stimulant.

### Sample Potassium Readings
### 276-5

Iodide of Potassium—acts directly to the *glands* of the body, specifically those glands relating to conditions (or a portion, or a system) in *eliminating* forces. Bromide of Potassium—rather a sedative, but such a *small* amount as to be a stimuli rather than sedative in its activity on the system. These elements will act *with* that outlined for the adjustment and manipulation osteopathically, in lumbar and sacral area—as well as in the upper cervical.

### 499-1 Reports

Potassium nourishes the muscular system, and heals injuries, reduces pain, balances the body and brain, causing versatility. Potassium attracts oxygen to the body, giving enthusiasm, activity, health, tone, and quick recuperative powers. Potassium is a curative, and when it is lacking the tissues and cells must be retrained to take it up by [eating a diet rich in natural plant foods], eliminating white flour, white sugar, pie, cake, pastry, and candy.

## *Silver*
### Ag
### Atomic Number 47

### History

Silver gets its chemical symbol from the Latin word for silver, *argentums*. Silver was important to the ancient Sumerians. Silver jewelry was found in graves there dating back to 3000 B.C. the Chaldeans were first to extract silver from its ore around 2500 B.C. Beginning around 900 B.C. the Larium mines near Athens, Greece were the biggest in the world for the next 1000 years. It is a favorite metal of alchemists and has been used as currency since biblical times. Later in the nineteenth century, silver became more affordable because of technological advancement and was popularized by Queen Victoria, who initiated the revival of Celtic designs in jewelry. Nevada produced millions of dollars in silver in the 1800s that continued into the twentieth century.

### Argentite—Silver Ore
### Ag2S

Silver is one of my favorite metals to wear. It is the metallic equivalent to the divine feminine and carries the healing energies of water to all who wear it. Silver also carries lunar energies and deals with secrets, the shadow self, or hidden talents and energies. It can be used to cool the body from fever, alleviate rashes and hives, and reduce swelling. If money is tight, silver can be used to assist you with collecting necessary funds to make ends meet. It creates a feeling of knowing that everything will be okay and there is plenty to go around. Silver is like the yin to the yang of gold, and because it is feminine, it is a nurturing energy that creates a feeling of emotional security, while its counterpart gold brings in aggressive masculine energy.

### Cayce Uses

Calms nerves when combined in a Cayce formula called Silver Nitrate.

### Sample Silver Readings
### 5500-1

While, as of those of the silver cord that makes for that transmutation of *impulse* from the brain to the  organs of the body, *sustaining*—as it were—that spark of life itself in a material plane.

### 1800-24 Reports

Silver nitrate is a nerve stimulant and would be beneficial in any condition relating to the nerves.

### 1800-24

(Q) Are there any particular fixed specifications for the following elements? Nickel silver: Its kind, percentage of Nickel and Copper and its temper?

(A) As indicated, the German Silver is preferable. Ordinary German Silver, or the German Silver for watch cases, you see; German Silver for platings that are used for the basis for silverware, or the like. Not plated, but just a German Silver.

### 1800-6

Many of the conditions as are existent in alcoholic stimulants, as have been applied to system, that has destroyed the tissue in central portion of the body, destroyed tissue in the re-creative forces in generatory system, destroyed tissue in other portions of the system, even into brain itself, give these, and gold or silver, or both, would add and rebuild, rejuvenate, as it were, in the system. Give these, for they are good.

### Biblical References

"For the merchandise of it is better than the merchandise of silver and the gain thereof than fine gold."

Proverbs 3:14

"The hooks of the pillars and their fillets of silver; and the overlaying of their chapiters of silver; and all the pillars of the court were filleted with silver."   Exodus 38:17

## *Sodium*
### Na
### Atomic Number 11

### History

Sodium is the sixth most abundant element on earth and an important element in seawater. Energetically it will help you connect with energies of the sea, and in healing it is a powerful tool to ward of negativity.

Aside from the salts you will read about below, one of my favorite ways to get the benefits of salt is with a salt lamp. The lamps create positive ionization in the air and bring a warm peaceful feeling to your home or office. Cayce often recommended different kinds of lamps for people to use, and salt lamps are gaining popularity and are an afford-able way to reap the benefits of light and sodium.

### Lye

In the readings, Cayce recommended lye be used for unwanted hair removal.

### 758-36

(Q) What is the condition of his eyes?
(A) These, as any other reaction from the sensory system, show the effect of irritations at times. More close attention should be paid to the bathing of the eyes morn-ing and evening with a solution that will cleanse them, see?
(Q) What solution would be suggested for this?
(A) A solution for the eyes; don't use lye or any of those things that are detrimental, but those that will work with the activities of the secretions themselves, see?

### 3341-1

(Q) I am especially anxious to find some treatment for the removal of superfluous hair which is on my body, espe-cially the face. I have tried electrolysis but the growth is too profuse to be removed successfully in this manner. Can you advise treatment for this condition?
(A) Better be glad you've got it, than to have other things that would cause a great deal more trouble by trying to remove same! But if ye pray right, live right, ask for it to be removed and ye may wash it off with lye soap.

### Baking Soda

In the readings, Cayce recommends a mixture of baking soda and castor oils to remove growths and warts, and to correct nerve damage from alcohol.

### 608-3

We would begin first (even with the cleansed system, in a manner) with broken doses of Castoria, after having flushed the system with two small doses of common baking soda, see? That is, this soda in the system—about a quarter to less than a quarter teaspoonful in three quarters glass of water. This will produce an alkaline condition in the system so that when the properties in Castoria are taken they produce a different effect on the body from that of entering an acid or a poison-ridden system.

### 1101-4

(Q) What is the best treatment for the corns on my left and right little toes?
(A) The application of a Soda and Spirits of Camphor solution. Wet the Baking Soda with Spirits of Camphor and massage these night and morning. In the evenings these may be bound with same. At first it will produce a little soreness, but after the second day this will disappear—the soreness. Then we will find the system, with the corrections osteopathically, will absorb—and these will disappear.

### Salts
### Table Salt
### NaCl

I have long been singing the praises of salt for a variety of medicinal and spiritual uses. It is important to understand that salts are not all created equal. Each variety has a totally different chemical structure and can do different things.

Aside from flavoring our food, common table salt can be used as a powerful protector of the energy field around your home. Take the salt-shaker or container outside and consciously sprinkle it around your house with the intention of placing a white light of protection around the entire perimeter of the property. Ask that the home and everyone in it be protected.

There is something very special about salt because for some reason, nothing negative can break through it. By protecting my home in this way, I have noticed fewer solicitors coming to the door, and the ones who do visit are very polite.

Once I was outside after dark with a salt container and a candle walking around the yard. My neighbor happened to notice me, yet said nothing. If he had asked, I could always say I was protecting the yard from the destructive habits of snails, which are also deterred by salt.

### Table Salt Readings
### 2871-1

Also, at least three times each week, just before retiring, take a good pinch of table salt dry on the tongue. Don't drink water afterwards. If it is necessary during the evening or night, this is well; but this will add sufficient to the salivary glands, to the condition in the stomach, as to prevent this entanglement that occurs oft in the sleep.

### 283-1

Massage the thumb, or the hand, or those extremities of the body that show there has been tautness in the muscular forces from the attempt to eradicate conditions, with equal parts, or a saturated solution, of salt and vinegar. This may be massaged into the hand once each day, or every other day—just so we overcome these conditions. Pure apple vinegar and saturated solution with salt—table salt, see?

### 779-8

Well that the body would use for this occasionally, when these become troublesome (as at present), equal parts of salt (common table salt), soda (baking soda) and Cream of Tartar in sufficient warm water that this may be snuffed up the nostril, until it is carried through to the mouth, and increase the length or time of the vibration from the violet ray forces along neck and back of neck,

and around throat. This, we see, will keep these eliminations going from the system, prevent the trouble re-oc-
curring in shoulder and in neck and trouble in throat. Do
that.

### Sea Salt

Sea salt is a powerful combination of bits and pieces of everything
that lives in the ocean. In fact, nearly every common element known on
earth is found within it and because of that, it is a very powerful healer
to the body when used in a bath. When you soak in this substance, all
the positive vibrations from all the sea creatures are absorbed in the
physical body. It is very restorative to the entire system.

Particularly those who are drawn to Atlantean past lives or the ocean
can greatly benefit from frequent exposure to sea salts.

Cayce mentioned sea salt 73 times in the readings.

### Sea Salt Readings
### 301-3

. . . respecting the menstrual periods. When these are severe, the use of hot packs—especially of heated heavy sea
salt—would be the greater relief for the body.

### 797-2

(Q) Is salt in diet injurious?
(A) Use kelp or deep sea salt instead of the regular table
salt.

### 4232-1

When the pain is severe across the back, or hips, it would
be well if the body would be sponged with a saturated solution of bicarbonate of soda and heat given in warm water of heated sea salt applied to this portion of the body.
Do that.

## Epsom Salt
### MgSO4

Epsom Salts are my personal favorite. They are inexpensive and easy to find. If you've ever had a sports-related injury you may have used Epsom salts to relieve your pain. They are excellent for reducing swelling and inflammation. They are also powerful and effective tools for raising your vibration by cleansing the aura. The magnesium is also good for you and this is one way to help you assimilate it quicker and easier.

## Epsom Salt Readings
### 5144-1

We would find that using daily Epsom Salt Packs would be very helpful. Take a hand and an arm on the same side of the body, wrap this in hot Epsom Salt water; this made almost a saturated solution. And this is to be followed by a rub, and rub toward the body at all times.

### 313-1

We would begin first with Epsom Salts packs, or baths. These we would take at least three times each week, for one week. If the packs are taken, saturated solution should be used—this applied over the lower portion of the spine, from the *sacral* region to that just above the kidney area—this applied as hot as the body may well stand, three times each week, one application at the time. Were this taken as salts baths, there would be about three to five pounds of salts in twenty gallons of water—this *warm*; or the salts dissolved in the tub, the body immersed in same, gradually *heat* the water by the addition of more hot water, see—slowly, as much as the body may stand. This will be more weakening than the packs, but would be *more active* in correcting the condition if the body *rests* for eight to ten hours after such ministration—see?

### Sodium and Your Pet

Pets can benefit from your use of salt, too. Have you ever noticed sometimes your pets suddenly react negatively to you and do not want to be near you? You may have noticed it always happens after you make a big change in yourself, or after a move. If you are going through a lot of energetic changes, that can be tough on your pet since your pet is really a mirror reflection of you. Help your pet out by sprinkling a tiny bit of table salt on their food or put some on your hand and have them lick it off. It helps them to integrate the changes they sense in you more quickly.

### Cayce Uses

Salts address everything from tight muscles, growths, and menstruation pain, according to Cayce.

### Sample Sodium Readings
### 1800-22

(Q) Should Calcium Chloride or Sodium Chloride be added to the sea water?
(A) Calcium Chloride.

### 3211-2

(Q) Shall I continue with my research work with dimethyl cellulose, sodium bicarbonate and salt solution?
(A) Continue with same. This will not be for a universal use, as indicated, but for the greater portion—yes.

## *Strontium*
### Sr
### Atomic Number 38

### History

In 1787 Strontium was first separated by William Cruikshank, and in 1790, Adair Crawford named it. Strontium is found in the ore of strontinite (SrCO3) and Celestite.

## Celestite
## SrSO4

Celestite is a beautiful stone that forms baby blue crystals currently found in Madagascar, off the coast of Africa. It is extremely dense and heavy. Spiritually it is said to have ties to angels, helping us communicate with them. It can also be used as a gift to give someone you love and respect, like a parent. I gave a piece to my mother for her birthday. In healing, I have used it to cleanse the energy fields of clients who I feel may have broken hearts. One particular case that comes to mind is a woman who was grieving her mother. Celestite can assist in the healing of grief and the mending and soothing of the heart.

### Cayce Uses

Used as a sedative.

### Sample Strontium Readings
### 279-17

(Q) Is the strontium bromide recently prescribed helping me, and should it be continued for the time suggested?
(A) As we find, this is rather the tendency for a too much of a sedative nature upon the nervous system.

## *Tin*
## Sn
## Atomic Number 50

### History

As early as 3500 B.C., bronze, an alloy of copper and tin, was used in ancient Egypt, making tin one of the first metals to be used by man. Pewter is a well-known alloy of tin, copper, antimony, and bismuth used widely by colonial settlers in the early Americas.

### Cayce Uses

Cayce sometimes recommended tin as a rustproof container for the remedies.

### Sample Tin Readings
### 1800-24

(Q) If cans were made of Tin, Brass, Copper or Zinc and Chromium plated after fabrication, would it be as satisfactory as the 18-8 Stainless metal?

(A) As indicated, make these of copper and tin, you see, so they do not rust.

### 1800-20

Stir well together. Preferable that this never be put in tin, but rather in the porcelain or glass . . .

### 1569-1

Put about a teaspoonful of the crushed seed in half a pint of boiling water, or pour the hot water on same, you see— in a crock container, *not* in tin or aluminum ware—and let it steep as ordinary tea, for ten to fifteen minutes. Then this taken warm, or as hot as the body can drink it, will be the more preferable.

## *Titanium*
### Ti
### Atomic Number 22
### Transition element

### History

Titanium is a silver–gray metal used as an alloy with iron and aluminum. It is found in Rutile and some iron ores. It is used to construct jet aircraft and medical equipment because it is lightweight and resistant to corrosion. Particularly within the past decade, Titanium bicycles have become more prevalent in competitive situations due to the lightweight nature of the material, yet they are extremely expensive. Titanium does not react with human tissue, making it an important metal in surgical pins used to repair broken bones.

### Titanium Crystal
### TiO2

Titanium is often electroplated on quartz and sold as crystals. The metal is interesting because when it combines with oxygen, it looks multi-colored, connecting you with the childlike joy of the rainbow spectrum. It can be used to supercharge and activate each of the seven primary chakra centers and bring tremendous energy and enthusiasm to any situation. It is a great gift for children.

### Rutilated Quartz

Rutile is a stringlike shiny metallic mineral and one of the only natural sources of Titanium. It is most often found in quartz deposits, often known as the "Hair of Venus." The gold-colored strings shoot out in all directions like Fourth of July fireworks, and will help you ignite new projects or endeavors. It can also help you get motivated to make a needed move and help you take the next step toward a major life change.

### Cayce Uses

Titanium shows up briefly because it was found as a trace element in a blood analysis. It was not mentioned much at all, but is an important element for you to consider using.

### Sample Titanium Readings
### 1564-2

*In the blood supply,* as we find, there are indications of there being the lack of the full purification of same through the pulmonary system. Spectographic analysis also shows present in trace amounts: barium, lithium, silicon, strontium, titanium, copper, boron.

# *Tungsten*
## W
### Atomic Number 74

### History

Tungsten is the product of two types of ore, Wolframite and Scheelite. It was discovered by two Spanish brothers Juan Jose and Fausto Elhuar in 1783 after isolating it from Wolframite. In some parts of the world, Tungsten is referred to as Wolfram, which is where the elemental symbol comes from, yet the origin of the name may be Swedish from the words *tung stem* which means "heavy stone."

Seventy-five percent of the worlds supply of Tungsten is thought to exist in China and because of that, this element reunites us with our past in Asia and can assist in healing any karmic blockages from those times. It can be particularly useful in aiding ailments of the feet, many of which are karmic and relate to a past life in which the feet were bound in aristocratic Asian cultures. The energy of wolframite helps the feet to expand, feeling free, and enables them to get the required circulation. Pains from bunions and bone spurs on the feet are also alleviated as the stone works to smooth out the sore spots and restore balance.

### Cayce Uses

Raises the vibration of the one using it.

### Sample Tungsten Readings
### 3099-1

These massages should be osteopathically administered, followed with an oil rub—using one part tungsten oil [GD's note: I think he means lamp oil or plain kerosene] and five parts peanut oil. Shake these thoroughly together and massage especially in those areas where the plates to the Appliance are attached to the body. This should be done at least every other day.

## 707-1

And attunement is made through such vibrations, just as there may be with the tungsten in a portion of a vacuum that may raise those sound waves that through their relativity of activity of the electrical vibration that makes for the activity of the atomic forces in same give that which is gathered from the ether waves. So may numbers and those vibrations from stones as given, with metals such as come in the lapis lazuli, make for the raising of the attunement in self through meditation. But know these, my child, are but means—and are *not* the God-Force, *not* the Spirit, but the *manifestations* of same.

# *Uranium*
## U
### Atomic Number 92

### History

Uranium is one of the heaviest metals. Uraninite, commonly referred to as Pitchblende, is the major ore for uranium and can be found in Colorado and Arizona, and in England, France, and Portugal.

### Radium (Ra)
### Atomic Number 88

Radium is an element formed by the decay of Uranium. Marie Curie isolated small amounts of radium from Pitchblende. It is highly radioactive and decays by emitting alpha, beta, and gamma radiation. Radium is used to kill cancer cells and is very toxic, easily destroying plant and animal cells.

### Radium Readings
### 1931-1

Hence the radial activity of radium, as well as the strengthening influences of gold the stabilizing influence of silver, are all a part of those elements that make for the transmission through the activity of the very vibratory forces themselves, and become to this body of great influence; for this entity is not only destined but rather prone to be thrown into those channels where all of such are necessary for usage in either the protection or destruction of mankind himself. As to which—the entity will choose, for it is within his own power.

### Cayce Uses

Cayce helped a man develop a new kind of furnace and spoke of radioactive elements in the process.

### Sample Uranium Readings
### 2431-1

(Q) Will you explain in a little more detail the laws of attraction and repulsion?
(A) There are atomic vibrations, and as there is the breaking up of each element in its forces and forms, there is produced the attraction or repulsion. As an illustration (this you can't use, so we will give it as an illustration): All of uranium elements are an attractive force for those influences that produce same, you see—platinum and all mercury products are attracted by uranium. Uranium, then, will indicate those locations of such pitchblende as would *produce some* form of its same elements, or platinum or platnite [?]. In the one—platinum—this would swing across, see? In the others—of the pitchblende—circular.

### 699-1

(Q) Will any success materialize for me from Salter's electric furnace?
(A) Uranium has something to do with it. Look to that end of separation—uranium; for you will find another element coming in, from the abilities of this electrical furnace, in this relationship. See? Not from the iron end, rather from the uranium—for we will make a new metal with this. Follow this out.

Perhaps Cayce was referring to the discovery of Curium in 1944, a radioactive element that can easily be converted into heat and electricity.

# *Vanadium*
## V
### Atomic Number 23

### History

Vanadium is an extremely toxic element used primarily in the steel industry, because as an alloy it makes very strong steel, and in the nuclear power industry, because of its strength resistance, to meld with other materials.

Originally discovered by Mexican mineralogy professor Andres Manuel del Rio in 1801, it gets its name from the Scandinavian goddess of youth and beauty, Vanadis, because of its many beautiful colors.

### Vanadinite

Several years ago, I picked up a beautiful vanadinite specimen that I have kept in my home office ever since. It is an excellent stone for people who are sensitive to psychic energy, or empathic. Empaths, as they are sometimes called, are people who easily and sometimes un-knowingly pick up energy from other people. Have you ever had an experience where you went into a meeting or party feeling great, then suddenly and seemingly out of nowhere began to feel sad, angry, or overwhelmed? This happened to me for many years until I finally real-ized what was going on. Because we are all connected at a spiritual level, it is easy to pick up what others are feeling. In healing work, this can be a gift, but if the gift is not treated properly or if you don't under-stand how to use it, you can become crippled by it. Vanadinite helps you to maintain your empathy and knowingness of what others are going through so that you can be of service to them, while keeping from literally "taking on" symptoms or feelings of others. You can know how people feel, yet you can maintain a boundary so that you are strong enough to offer the help that is truly needed.

### Cayce Uses

There are a few mentions of Vanadium in the Spectrographic Analysis of some of the patients, and other readings referred to the stock market and probably to the Vanadium Corporation of America, a prominent company in the 1930s that was run by Prescott Bush, grandfather of President George W. Bush.

Vanadium comes from the ore of Carnotite, which is listed in the following reading report:

"The Radio-Active Solar Pad is carefully constructed on scientific principles and consists of a heavy felt backing with a prepared rubber facing. The face of the Pad is treated with several coats of finely ground, high-grade Carnotite ore, Radium Barium Sulphate and Radiofied Calcium Sulphide." (1866-8 Reports)

### Sample Vanadium Readings
### 2708-6

In the *present* situation, we find these—especially the R.K.O. and Vanadium will prove to be exceptionally good holdings, can they be held to until there is the general change as must soon begin, and were they held—even at this very low figure, even bought much higher—these will prove exceptional holdings.

## *Zinc*
### Zn
### Atomic Number 30

### History

Zinc may have been used as early as the fifteenth century in India. Commercially it is used as a corrosion-resistant coating. Surprisingly, since 1981, the U.S. penny, although coated in copper to maintain its traditional look, is primarily made of zinc. Today zinc is an important trace element required for healthy plants and animals, and it can be found naturally in proteins such as fish, meat, eggs, and milk.

## Zincite
## ZnO

Zincite comes primarily from a huge mine in New Jersey, although it can be found elsewhere; the New Jersey location is so abundant, it caused zincite to quickly become a primary ore of zinc. Zincite allows the body to absorb nutrients from protein and can help rebuild healthy tissue and muscle. It builds stamina both mentally and physically.

## Smithsonite
## ZnCO3

Zinc is often extracted from the ore of Smithsonite, a zinc-carbonate. Smithsonite can be used to clear blockages in the heart and throat centers, fight the common cold and build the immune system. It is found in various parts of Africa, Greece, Russia, Turkey, and in Colorado and New Mexico.

One of my dear friends gave me the most beautiful piece of Smithsonite from the Magdalena mines in New Mexico. She said it opened up her crown chakra and cleared her energy field. I agree. This is a peaceful stone with a beautiful loving energy that will help you connect with your source, and the gentle green color it emanates will help heal deep emotions and bring inner peace and harmony.

## Cayce Uses

Recommended repeatedly for use in rash, dermatitis, shingles, eczema, psoriasis, and acne.

## Sample Readings
## 2015-2

For the rash, we would dust same with the Stearate of Zinc Powder with Balsam.

## 849-43

When the solution refuses to make a spark or charge, in making short circuit at the poles, recharge; using the greater amount of the zinc . . . (849-43) The solution for charging the Appliance should be at least double strength, as indicated; that is, instead of the one and a half pounds to the gallon and a half of water, use three pounds. The zinc also would be doubled . . . (849-48) For, without sufficient of the acid *and* of the zinc, the others will not produce the proper vibrations. (849-61)

# Non-Metals

## *Arsenic*
### As
### Atomic Number 33

### History

Arsenic has an illustrious history, immortalized in the film *Arsenic and Old Lace* with Cary Grant about two women who poison their houseguests. It has been a great theme of many mystery writers. As little as one-tenth of a gram of this element is enough to kill, and amazingly, it was only recently that it could be detected in an autopsy, so many poisonings could have potentially gone unnoticed.

### Arsenopyrite

This is the major ore of arsenic and is currently flooding the gem-stone markets. Arsenopyrite is made of arsenic combined with gold as an impurity. As different minerals are broken down, arsenopyrite is often discovered, and separating the arsenic from the gold, produces most of the world's supply of arsenic.

Because this amazing mineral contains the power of gold with the deadly poison arsenic, you can use the stone to repel negativity from you while you reach for a higher ideal. There are times when you may find yourself working on a project so dear to you that if you speak of it the energy of it may be ruined. Arsenopyrite can assist you in protecting the idea while allowing it to come to fruition and reach its highest potential.

### Cayce Uses

Recommended for circulation, digestion, and kidney and liver cleansing.

## Sample Arsenic Readings
### 984-2

*In the blood supply,* we find there is a heaviness and a lack of the activities through the circulation in the liver, as well as in the lungs, for the better or the more perfect purification of same.

First we would begin with very small doses of Fowler's Solution of Arsenic.

The solution of Arsenic in the manner indicated acts upon not only the whole of the respiratory system but the liver *and* the kidneys as combined with the gastric flow from the gall duct, the pancreas and the spleen, in their activity to assimilation and digestion.

### 1360-1

(Q) Has this body been taking arsenic or any other poison deliberately or unaware?
(A) Aware of those as taken. The arsenic is more as an acetate of arsenic, or that which is in a solution for thinning blood. This is more deliberate.

### 992-2

(Q) Are there any recommendations for the diet, other than that which is being followed?
(A) Let there be a tendency towards that of the vegetables being such as carry those of arsenic or such cleansing forces in the system, which are of the *silicon* derivatives—see?
(Q) What are these vegetables, or those that carry these properties?
(A) Onions, leeks, lentils, spinach, carrots (especially raw); the more of these that are taken raw, the better it would be.

### 349-10

With the conditions that disturb the body, the food values will have much to do with creating—with these properties' activity—the proper blood coordination in the system. As is understood, arsenic is a slow poison, in small quantities, as this, but it is also an element that will work with the gastric forces in the duodenum, and especially in the lacteal glands.

# *Boron*
## B
### Atomic Number 5

### History

Sir Humphrey Davy, the English chemist who is credited with discovering seven other elements, isolated boron from its ore in 1808. Boron is never found pure in nature. It is unusual because it is considered a non-metal, yet it behaves like metal. It is used in industry as a booster for rocket fuel, an alloy for many metals, in fiberglass insulation, and in transistors. In pyrotechnics, boron is used to produce a green color. Cosmetics, water softeners, and soaps also contain boron in the form of the substance known as borax, which is a mild antiseptic.

### Cayce Uses

Boracic acid, as well as the Irish potato, is mentioned repeatedly throughout the readings as an external remedy for eye irritations or blindness. It was also recommended to relieve potentially infectious skin abrasions, dermatitis, and toxemia, and occasionally prescribed as an enema for intestinal problems.

### Sample Boron Readings
### 3741-1

Reduce the condition in cuticle by using the properties as would be found in chalk and of boracic acid to prevent the irritation, equal parts rubbed on body when irritation is severe.

### 4749-2

(Q) Should the Boracic Acid Wash be used with the Listerine for the throat?
(A) That is what we have given. That is what we mean, that this should be used with it.

### 934-10

Use the warm Boracic Acid Solution, preferably in eye cup, about twice a day.

## *Chlorine*
### Cl
### Atomic Number 17

### History

Chlorine is a poisonous gas naturally occurring mostly in dissolved salts in seawater and salt mine deposits. It was first seen by Carl Wilhelm Scheele of Sweden in 1774, but was not properly identified as an element until English chemist Sir Humphrey Davy did so in 1810. The name chlorine is from the Greek word *chloros*, meaning greenish yellow.

### Chlorine Quartz
### ClSO2

New on the gem market this year, chlorine quartz is coming into its own in the healing community. It is interesting to see this and the Lithium quartz taking such a role in healing now. I think this is a result of earth changes and the need to get back to basics at a deep subconscious level. This stone will cleanse you energetically, washing away all the old stuff, so you may be refreshed and ready to ascend to higher spiritual places in the coming years.

### Cayce Uses

Recommended as a rinse for the mouth to prevent tooth decay.

### Sample Chlorine Reading
### 2981-2

(Q) Give care of teeth so I will have less decaying?

(A) Use as a massage for the gums and teeth an equal combination of common table salt and baking soda; about once a month, add one drop only of chlorine to a pint of water and rinse the mouth with this. Do not swallow it, but rinse the mouth and then brush the teeth. This will preserve them, even aid in filling cavities.

## *Fluorine*
### F
### Atomic Number 9

### History

Although Flourine was first discovered in the late 1700s, Henri Moissan of France was the first person to create an elemental form of fluorine and won the nobel prize for his efforts in 1906. Fluorine is used in the dental industry as Sodium Fluoride, a key ingredient in toothpaste. It is also artificially linked with carbon to produce Teflon used in non-stick cookware.

### Fluorite
### CaF2

Fluorite, also known as calcium fluoride, is one my favorite minerals. It will help you focus and concentrate on complex issues and ideas and can serve as a relief for severe allergy sufferers. If you lay down and place raw fluorite on your sinus cavities, located on each side of your nose below your eyes, sinuses will drain and headaches will be relieved, and the positive byproduct is increased ability to concentrate after you wake up from the experience.

These days, most fluorite, as well as many other colored gems, are mined primarily in Brazil, although southern Colorado has some spectacular fluorite specimens.

## Cayce Uses

September 14, 1943, Cayce gave a reading to the man who may have invented Flouride toothpaste.

### Sample Fluorine Reading
### 3211-1

(Q) Regarding the universal approach: Is it true, as it is thought, that the intake of certain form and percentage of fluorine in drinking water causes mottled enamel of the teeth?

(A) This, to be sure, is true; but this is also untrue unless there is considered the other properties with which such is associated in drinking water. If there are certain percents of fluorine with free limestone, we will find it is beneficial.

(Q) Does too much fluorine cause decay of teeth, and where is the borderline?

(A) Read what has just been indicated. It depends upon the combinations, more than it does upon the quantity of fluorine itself. There are many sections, of course, where fluorine added to the water, with many other chemicals would be most beneficial. There are others where, even a small quantity added would be very detrimental.

(Q) Is the paste of sodium fluorine and lime that I have prepared safe to use for desensitizing erosion cavities, and could we seal it in cavities for desensitizing same, for drilling out decay and preparing teeth for restoration?

(A) It could be used in ninety percent of the conditions.

## *Helium*
### He
### Atomic Number 2

### History

Helium (Greek for "helios" or sun) is unusual because it always exists in elemental form and cannot combine with anything, going completely undetected due to its colorless and odorless state. Next to hydrogen, helium is the second most abundant element in the universe, making up seven percent of all atoms. The mineral uraninite, an ore of uranium and radium, produces helium.

Helium gives the gift of independence and the strength and courage to stand tall for convictions, the independence to work alone, and a feeling of being okay with solitude. Personal fulfillment, laughter and joy surround this light airy element. The laughter helium brings when it alters your vocal chords reminds you to play, have fun, and not to take yourself too seriously.

### Cayce Uses

Cayce spoke about helium when describing a possible structure for air ships used in Atlantis.

### Sample Helium Reading
### 195-70

As is seen at present, helium becomes the greater usage in containers that may be made; yet these *themselves* (This is working from the opposite side, see?)—but were those gases, or those metals used that the supply of helium itself becomes the container *for* the vacuum itself, see? this condensed, see? into a metal form, *then* the vacuum may be made that would lift without being lifted, see?

# *Iodine*
## I
### Atomic Number 53

### History

Iodine is made from ashes of burned seaweed. It is an extremely reactive purple colored gas named from the Greek word *iodes*, meaning "violet-colored." It is not found at all in the mineral kingdom, yet you can still tap into its energies through solutions such as those listed below.

Like the Phoenix bird that rose from the ashes, this is an element of renewal from fire and will connect you with the deepest recesses of the earth and the secrets of the ocean itself.

## Cayce Uses

Atomic Iodine solution (Atomidine) alleviates high blood pressure, and Cayce recommended diets filled with iodine to assist the nervous system.

## Sample Iodine Readings
### 813-2

There is a lack of the necessary forces for keeping a full flow of the normal corpuscle activity, owing to the lack of the elements in the body—and the blood supply—for the balance between the iodine and potash. Or there is an excess of potash in the system.

### 1125-2

. . . iodine—which in this formula or in this manner (Atomidine) is non-poisonous, non-toxic, but is healing to mucous membranes, is an astringent and a healer and a purifier of tissue in the body. Use such a weak spray whenever there are the irritations arising through the sinus and the antrums.

### 499-1 Reports

Principal Iodine Foods: Iodine sea lettuce, raw egg in orange juice, Cod liver oil, smoked salmon, skin of baked potato, Irish moss, lobster, artichokes, strawberries, green grapes, frogs' legs, oysters, shrimp, green turtle, mushrooms, onions, tomatoes, clams, pineapple, crawfish, crabs, scallops, garlic, peas, pears.

Iodine is the great protector of the brain and nervous system from body toxins. Lack of iodine means extreme nervousness, erratic notions, and worries. Iodine stimulates the glands, balances the weight, causes assimilation of calcium and blood salts, increases oxygen assimilation, balances and increases brain activity. All people need iodine. No temperaments have iodine in excess. Those who need it the most, however, are the anemic, emotional, nervous, sentimental, easily upset temperaments, and also those with goitre and tendency to nervous prostration. Big heads and puny bodies, diabetic and nephritic types, those with unnecessary fears and apprehensions, squinting eyes, alternate talking spells and stupor, flabby lower abdomen, awkward movements, soggy head colds, excessive hunger feeling rather than very full sensations, frothy saliva, numbness, irritation from the sun, lack of concentration—these symptoms and many others of a "nervous" nature are not due to "imagination." They need iodine. There is no such thing as "just nerves."

## *Nitrogen*
### N
### Atomic Number 7

### History
Chemistry student Daniel Rutherford discovered nitrogen in 1772 after experimenting with a candle. He covered it and realized that after the oxygen had burned out that another gas was present. Nitrogen is an asphyxiant because it takes oxygen out of the air, and it is the most common gas in the earth's atmosphere.

### Nitratine
### NaNO3
Nitrogen is not common in the mineral kingdom, but does occur occasionally in a sodium nitrate form called nitratine, a very delicate mineral that will actually turn to liquid after absorbing water from the air. Because of that, this stone will help you if you are overly emotional or have a lot of water planets in your astrological chart and need to remain calm, cool, and collected.

## Cayce Uses

Nitrogen is used in the production of Carbon Ash, a common Cayce remedy.

### Sample Nitrogen Readings
### 165-15

(Q) In producing the ash, may the other elements in the air consist of a gas such as acetylene?
(A) Not too much of it. More of the *natural* gases of the air is better in the product. That of the hydrogen, nitrogen, oxygen—these are better in the air than the gases as would come from acetylene.

### 928-1

(Q) Any advice as to diet of the mother?
(A) Keep a diet well-balanced or well-rounded in iron, nitrogen, and the necessary bone structural forces in the activities that arise from such diets. Milk, a good vegetable diet; not acid-forming foods, not too heavy of meats—but a well-rounded, well-balanced diet.

### 2710-3

(Q) What is the cause of frequent colds and headaches?
(A) . . . the pressure as is produced on the sphlenic [splenic?] nerves and the active forces to the gall *bladder* especially, or gall ducts—these prevent that being carried in the system that is able, through the assimilation of food values, to create the plasm necessary in the blood supply to cope with the germ when it enters the system— which is, as is known, as prevalent in the air as is oxygen, or nitrogen, or hydrogen.

Treatment for a man with a parasitic infection:

### 4444-2

(Q) What is the niccolite composed of?

(A) Oxygen, nitrogen, and action on the force of putrified matter in the animal; in the state we have it from the animal matter, acted on by nature, or put there by its Maker for the use of mankind when he needs it. This man needs it, take it and use it.

## *Oxygen*
### O
### Atomic Number 8

### History

One of the most abundant elements on earth, oxygen is essential to life. It is a key component in the air we breathe, the water in our bodies and on our planet, and is part of most minerals on earth.

Spiritually, oxygen reminds us to breath, to take in the richness of life and all it has to offer. It is an energy of pure emotion because breathing is a very emotional experience. When you breathe, you feel things, you smell things, and those smells go straight to the brain stem, to the oldest part of the brain and remind you of things past.

Oxygen allows us to be at our ideal weight and body size. Proper breathing can help burn necessary calories for weight loss, or it can allow the cells to expand to assist the body in achieving perfect health.

When you breathe out of your mouth, as I used to do, the sympathetic nervous system is activated and the adrenal glands go into affect creating a fight or flight response. That would be okay if you were living in prehistoric times and needed to run to hunt food, or escape the deathly grips of a predator. These days, there is no need to use the adrenals to a great extent, yet we do it all the time and it ultimately wears the body down. Cayce mentions the sympathetic nervous system hundreds of times in the readings:

> These as we find produce disturbances between the cerebrospinal and the sympathetic nervous system coordination.                                              1572-1

The cerebrospinal nervous system is most likely another name for the parasympathetic nervous system. It controls rest and relaxation and digestion. If you do not breathe out of your nose, this system will not get activated and digestive problems will occur. Of all the life readings, elimination problems make up an extremely high percentage of problems people had in Cayce's time, and if you take a look at commercials on TV lately, you will see this problem has only gotten worse. Dozens of digestion–related products flood the market each year. Many of these ailments could be alleviated through proper breathing.

### Cayce Uses
As mentioned above, most of the 537 oxygen readings deal with the proper intake of oxygen as it is applied to healing all sorts of ailments within the body.

### Sample Oxygen Readings
### 632-17
(Q) How long will it be necessary to continue oxygen?
(A) Until the blood has sufficiently rehabilitated itself to carry on the eliminations through their nominal channels, or until there is a disintegration in some portions.

### 1734-5
While oxidized, or oxygen is also a necessary element in the breaking up, especially of tissue that is infected in any manner in the human body . . .

## *Phosphorus*
### P
### Atomic Number 15

### History
Discovered in 1669, Phosphorus is an element that is essential to life. In the spirit of alchemy, German chemist Hannig Brand made an attempt to turn urine into gold and discovered phosphorus instead. It is a white powder that glowed in air and is named the Greek word for *"light bearer."*

## Cayce Uses
Recommended to relax the body.

### Sample Phosphorus Readings
### 255-3
(Q) Specify foods containing phosphorus?
(A) The yolk of egg, none of the white. Those in carrots, celery, turnips, *all* carry a form of phosphorus that are additions, and solubles to the system. Milk also, if warm with the animal heat. That which has been pasteurized does not carry same.

Those (foods) of the silicon, and those that act *with* the phosphorus, for the activity of the glands in system, in evening. *These* will rest the body.

### 1173-8
(Q) Would phosphorus be helpful to him? If so, will you suggest the name of a tonic including phosphorus and iron?
(A) As we find, phosphorus, to be sure, is a necessary element, but its assimilation from synthetic concoctions is oft hard upon the body. The assimilation of same from food values then becomes much more not only palatable but activative with the influences of the body. Those then as we find of the artichoke, the lowly rutabaga or turnip—these taken at least once to twice a week as a portion of the meal—will be the better manner for this to be assimilated by this body at the present time.

## *Silicon*
### Si
### Atomic Number 14

### History
The second most abundant element next to oxygen, silicon is a prime component of some of the most common minerals on earth.

The power of silicon cannot be underestimated. It is a critical part of the mineral kingdom comprising parts of so many stones, I could not name them all here. Silicon brings speed and clarity to the healing process. It is like a rocket booster that amps up the speed and quickens everything it touches.

## Quartz
### SiO2

Quartz, named after a Slavic word for "hard," is the crystalline form of silicon, and many of the gems, such as clear crystal, amethyst, citrine, tiger's eye, aventurine, and carnelian, are from the quartz family.

Each type of quartz brings different energies, but as a family of gems, quartz stones represent transition and change. They transmit a high frequency that brings about smooth yet often rapid changes in health or general conditions.

### Quartz Readings

Quartz is mentioned by name 141 times in the readings, primarily as used in mercury–quartz lamps for the treatment of arthritis, hemorrhage, pleurisy, cancer, multiple sclerosis, tumors, tuberculosis, body-building, spinal issues, and ulcers.

### 5609-2

(Q) Would the Sun-Lamp Quartz or Carbon help eliminations and general condition? If so, state manner of treatment.

(A) These may be given occasionally, but should not be a continued portion of the treatment. They assist and stimulate, especially when there are movements made in the muscular forces, where the activities come from impulses in centers along the cerebro-spinal system.

### Flint

Flint is non–crystalline form or crystal used in ancient times to start fires. Flint is also a stone of transition and rapid change, often assisting energetically with completely bringing down old systems or ways of doing things to make way for the new. It brings change so swiftly and without emotion that it feels a bit heartless, but by not allowing you to get too tied up in reminiscing over past events, flint encourages you to think positively and anticipate a brighter future knowing that you have to give up things to get better things down the road.

### Flint Readings
There are a few mentions of flint in the readings, most talking about geological elements within land.

### 3656-1
In Uranus we find that the entity may be very magnanimous in some experience and then as hard as flint in another.

### Cayce Uses
Recommended to regenerate organs and systems of the body and to assist better functioning of glands.

### Sample Silicon Reading
### 255-3
(Q) Those [foods] containing silicon.
(A) These are found in beets, carrots, spinach. In such these may be found.

### 1000-1
Beware, then, of starches and of sugars—but add as much of those that will carry the more *stabilizing* conditions for the system, in silicon, gold, and of those that *regenerate* the whole of the system as related to the *glands*.

## Sulfur
### S
### Atomic Number 16

### History
Sulphur in mineral form is bright yellow, and can be found near hot

springs, geysers, and some volcanoes. Gypsum and Pyrite are common sulfur-based minerals.

Energetically sulphur deeply cleanses the system of toxins both physically and etherically and aids not only in "burning off" unwanted conditions, but spiritually ridding you of unwanted situations. A powerful psychic protection stone, sulfur keeps negative thoughts from penetrating the aura and causing misfortune. Around the home, it can be used to create a wall of protection around your property simply by placing pieces in four corners around the home. They energetically link together to create a strong protective force that cannot be broken.

### Cayce Uses

Cayce recommended a mixture called Balsam of Sulfur for treatment of elimination problems, arthritis, paralysis, lesions, circulation, spleen psoriasis, toxemia, dermatitis, scoliosis, boils, and any kind of nervous system disorder.

### Sample Sulfur Readings
### 4630-2

(Q) How much Balsam of Sulfur should be massaged into the body at a time?
(A) About what would be held in the hand, see? See, the Balsam of Sulfur is Sulfur boiled in oil, and is of a dark mealy, or liquid—heavy—of this combination, see?

### 136-74

Using those properties as given—the sulphur, the cream of tartar, and salts—see? These in small quantities, taken properly as given, will cleanse the condition, see?

# Part Three

# Gems, Stones, and Minerals

(Q) Is there a stone or ring somewhere waiting for me, that I should wear? What causes the feeling that there is, and what power has such a stone in reference to one's life?

(A) The ruby would make for the body that not as something which would be other than the power that self attributes to same, through its actual experience. But the light or reflection from same, worn on hand or body, will enable the body to concentrate in its mental application the greater—through the influences such a stone brings to material expression.

How? Each element, each stone, each variation of stone, has its own atomic movement, held together by the units of energy that in the universe are concentrated in that particular activity. Hence they come under varied activities according to their color, vibration or emanation. In this particular one (the ruby) there is that fitness with that which has been the experience of *this* soul, this entity, through material expression. Hence it is an aid, a crutch to lean upon. But, as has always been given, let it be a stepping-stone; *not* that which thou *standest* only upon!

# The Dream Continues . . .

Several months had passed since my strange dream about the *Maltese Falcon*. I read the book and watched the wonderful film with Humphrey Bogart. The book had one section I was particularly drawn to:

> "Mr Joel Cairo was a small-boned dark man of medium
> height. His hair was black and smooth and very glossy.
> His features were Levantine. A square-cut ruby, its sides
> paralleled by four baguette diamonds, gleamed against
> the deep green of his cravat . . . Cairo turned his hat over,
> dropping his gloves into it, and placed it bottom up on
> the corner of the desk nearest him. Diamonds twinkled
> on the second and fourth fingers of his left hand, a ruby
> that matched the one in his tie even to the surrounding
> diamonds on the third finger of his right hand . . . a plati-
> num Longines watch on a platinum and red gold chain . . . a
> silver and onyx fountain-pen . . . "

On another night, several months later, I found myself back in
the same dream in the darkened cavern, standing with Cayce as
he extended his arm back in a welcoming gesture, revealing
thousands of precious gems: rubies, sapphires, emeralds, and
diamonds.

"Look," he said. "The gems!"

As I looked behind him, I saw huge treasure chests filled with many
of the gems featured in the *Maltese Falcon*. I thought I understood what it
all meant, until some time later, when I realized the dream was not over
and there was much more to see and to experience. For now, though, I
knew I had to explore these gems—the gems Cayce mentioned in his
work.

# Stones of the Bible

## *Breastplate of the High Priest*

"And thou shalt set in it settings of stones, even four rows
of stones: the first row shall be a sardius, a topaz and a
carbuncle: this shalt be the first row.

"And the second row shall be an emerald, a sapphire, and a diamond.

"And the third row a ligure, an agate and an amethyst.

"And the fourth row a beryl, and an onyx, and a jasper; they shall be set in gold in their inclosings.

"And the stones shall be with the names of the children of Israel, twelve, according to their names, like the engravings of a signet; every one with his name shall they be according to the twelve tribes." Exodus 28:17-21

"Thou hast been in Eden the garden of God; every precious stone was thy covering, the sardius, topaz, and the diamond, the beryl, the onyx, and the jasper, the sapphire, the emerald, and the carbuncle, and gold: the workmanship of thy tablets and of thy pipes was prepared in thee in the day that thou wast created." Ezekiel 28:13

The breastplate of the High Priest is an important part of the Edgar Cayce readings. The stones of the breastplate represent the twelve tribes of Israel. Cayce mentions the breastplate three times:

The entity then was among the daughters of Levi, and those chosen to make the vestment of the priest. And to the entity, because of its own abilities, there was given the preparation of the settings of the breastplate and the putting of the stones thereon, and the preparation of the Urim and Thummim for the interpretations of the movements that came upon the high priest in the holy of holies to be given to his people in or from the door of the tabernacle. 987-2

Put ye on, then, the whole armor of God, the breastplate of righteousness, the sword of the spirit of truth.
1747-5

Thus again it may be said that the entity should let that

shield be a reminder to self to put on the whole armor of
God, acquitting self as a good soldier; keeping that breastplate of righteousness, the feet shod as with good tidings
ever.                                                      1877-2

Extensive research into the exact identity of the stones in the breastplate still baffles scholars from all over the world. The challenge comes
from several factors. First, the language translations over thousands of
years presupposes that some meanings are bound to be lost or misinterpreted. Second, geological factors have to be considered as far as
what mineral deposits are likely to occur in the areas where biblical
history unfolded.

The biblical passages above were taken from the King James Version
of the Bible. The New International Version offers an entirely different
view of the stones in the breastplate:

"In the first row there shall be a ruby, a topaz and a beryl;
in the second row a turquoise, a sapphire and an emerald;
in the third row a jacinth, an agate and an amethyst;
in the fourth row a chrysolite, an onyx and a jasper."

As you can see, in this version, there are some discrepancies as ruby,
turquoise, and chrysolite are mentioned. For that reason, and because
there are so many versions of the Bible out now, each with a different
interpretation of these stones, with each entry I have included all the
possible identities for that particular stone and will discuss each one
and share my opinion on the true identity. You can take a look and
decide for yourself. The King James Version will always be listed first.

I wanted to include the listing of the tribes next to the stone that
each represents, but that too leads to a scholarly debate and no two
opinions are alike. The book of Numbers gives the name of each tribe
as follows: Reuben, Simeon, Gad, Judah, Issachar, Zebulun, Joseph,
Manasseh (half-tribe), Benjamin, Dan, Asher, Naphtali, and Levi (priests).
(Numbers 1:26–50)

## Row One

### Sardius/Sardonyx/Red Carnelian, Ruby

Scholars are split down the middle about the identity of the first stone of the breastplate. Historically, it has been known as sardius, another term for carnelian, yet today there are many people who believe ruby to be the true identity of this stone. This is a tough one to call because there are two ways to look at it.

First, ruby was actually named in two other places in the Bible, so in some respects I find it hard to believe the translation would not have been consistent throughout. On the other side of that argument, a book as old as the Bible that has been translated as many times as it has by so many different people could account for the discrepancy. Scholars who support ruby as the first breastplate stone do so because of geological factors and the likelihood of the stone being present in the area during that time in history.

Through muscle testing, I am inclined to believe the true identity of the first stone is ruby. You can decide for yourself.

## *Sardius/Sardonyx/Red Carnelian*
### SiO2
### Carnelian or Sard

### History and Healing Uses

Carnelian, also known as Sard or Sardonyx in ancient times, is one of the most important gemstones in history. It was used to adorn the robe of Sumerian Queen Pu–Abi in the third century B.C. Ancient Egyptians believed carnelian ensured the passage of the soul into the next world; Greeks and Romans used it to make cameos and carved rings; and Goethe said it brought good luck and protected people from evil.

I have found carnelian to be an amazing psychic protection stone. I wear it often when I am in large crowds of people so I do not pick up their energy or allow others energy to wear me down.

It is also great for allergies. This was reported to me by a friend who said it cleared up her sinuses, and later on a trip to Colorado where there tends to be a lot of pollen floating around, I was at a shop doing a workshop and handed a student a piece of carnelian. She immediately got a strange look on her face and when I asked her what was wrong she said, "Nothing's wrong, I just can't believe this! My nose started to clear up as soon as I held this stone."

Some people find carnelian helps insomnia. I believe that is because of the protective nature of the stone. You can definitely sleep soundly when you know you are safe.

Vibrationally speaking, carnelian is the carrier of the orange ray, which activates and opens the second or sacral chakra. This means that it is a stone of creativity, sexuality, and material abundance.

### Cayce Uses

Cayce never mentioned carnelian by its modern name, but did mention sardonyx to be used to enhance the vibration of one of his clients, and to describe a past life.

### Sample Sardis/Sardonyx Readings
### 1528-1

Well that there be carried on the person the sardonyx stone (that is, in its semi-precious state); either in statuettes, pins, buttons, or a piece of same carried. Not as a protection but rather for the vibratory forces that influence the choices made by the mental forces of the entity itself.

### 294-148

Also in the land now known as Abyssinia, and those portions yet undiscovered or used in the upper lands of the river Nile, there were those mines of the precious stones—as onyx, beryl, sardis, diamond, amethyst, opal, and the pearls that came from the sea near what is now called Madagascar.

# *Ruby*
## Al203

### History

Ruby is an amazing stone—one of the most powerful stones on our planet. It has graced the heads of kings and has been a favorite of many people for eons.

Ruby is vibrating at the same frequency as the red ray and is used for healing the heart both physically and emotionally. It is a stone of deep love and is a wonderful gift to give to those you love.

### Ruby Zoisite—
### AlO3Ca2Al3(SiO4)3(OH)

Ruby Zoisite ( also called anyolite) is a wonderful stone just emerging into the gem healing community. Deposits of ruby are being found inside a stone called zoisite, an interesting bright green mineral with black hornblende specks. The result is a stone that looks like a watermelon. Like all green and red stones, this one holds the amazing heart healing properties of ruby, amplified by the soothing green zoisite. Aside from its unusual beauty, this stone is particularly useful in treating physical ailments of the heart such as clogged arteries and angina.

### Cayce Uses

Cayce said ruby imparts valor and strength to those who use it.

### Sample Ruby Readings
### 630-2

Also there were in the experience those things that make for what is ordinarily termed or considered royalty; as brocaded goods, gold, laces, pearls, rubies, etc. And *innately* has the entity builded in itself visions of many of those things that pertained to the royal robes, the ermines, the large hooks and crooks that went with such, in the ways of walking and activity in the various relationships of groups and individuals.

## 2916-1

Peoples, things—their positions, their qualifications, interest the entity. The abilities as a judge of cloth, furs, and values, are a part of the entity's experience from that material sojourn; also its interest in stones—especially pearls and rubies.

## 1144-2

These should be the colors about the entity, as should be the stones of the ruby and the pearl. For these have their influences; the purity of the pearl, though under stress it may come into being; the valor and the strength that is imparted in the inner influence of the ruby about the body.

## 531-3

The ruby would make for the body that not as something which would be other than the power that self attributes to same, through its actual experience, but the light or reflection from same (ruby) worn on hand or body, will enable the body to concentrate in its mental application the greater though the influences such a stone brings to material expression.

### Biblical References

"She is more precious than rubies: and all the things thou canst desire are not compared unto her."     Proverbs 3:15

"For wisdom is better than rubies; and all the things that may be desired are not to be compared to it."

Proverbs 8:11

### Topaz, Chrysolite, Jade

There are so many different varieties of topaz, it is not unreasonable to assume it could be misinterpreted as chrysolite (modernly known as peridot) or jade. Jade is historically linked to China, although it is interesting to note the area known as Turkistan, or what is modernly called

Turkey/Pakistan area, is famed for amazing jade deposits and has been heavily influenced by the Chinese. In fact, the west part of the Great Wall is known as Yu Min Guang, meaning Jade Gate, and faces the jade-producing Turkistan territory. If you have the opportunity to visit Turkey, or Asia Minor, you will see the Asian architectural influences there are still strong today. Therefore, the theory that jade could be a stone in the breastplate is certainly valid. My thoughts on this is that it may not be the replacement for topaz as various Bibles suggest, but could actually be a replacement for emerald, listed later in the breastplate.

## *Topaz*
### Al2SiO4(F,OH)2

### History

Topaz comes from the Sanskrit word for "fire," and has been used since ancient times. Ancient Egyptians believed it carried the golden rays of the sun god Ra, making it a particularly important protective amulet. The Greeks thought it could make a person invisible in times of danger, and topaz supposedly changed color to warn people if food or drink was poisoned.

The most famous and important topaz is a clear cut piece set in a crown of Portugal called the Braganza Diamond because this 1680 carat topaz was once mistaken for a diamond. The Smithsonian also has some huge faceted topaz specimens in the National Gem Collection worth seeing. Topaz is a tough stone, yet has the ability to easily fracture along cleavage points so great care must be taken during setting. Topaz ranges in color from light blue, green, yellow, and pink, depending on other minerals in the stone.

Topaz brings an energy of playfulness and joy into your life. Its bright pastel colors resonate with the season of spring, renewal, and hope. Use topaz any time you need to make a fresh start. It will give you the energy and clarity to make it a smooth and happy transition.

### Cayce Uses

Once again, Cayce is recommending this stone for the vibrational benefit of the seeker. Topaz brings so much light and joy to people, it would surely lift the spirit of anyone who uses it.

### Sample Topaz Readings
### 2120-1

These colors, as we find, are especially those that tend to-wards those of the opal, or the topaz, and *in* these—these; for the entity *made* same those of the scarabs that later became sacred to those peoples.

### 2281-1

Keep the topaz as a stone about thee always. Its beauty, its purity, its clarity, may bring to thee strength. For this ye have found, and will find oft needed in thy dealings with thy problems, and with thy fellow men.

### Biblical References

"The topaz of Ethiopia shall not equal it, neither shall it be valued with pure gold." Job 28:19

## *Chrysolite/Peridot*
### (Mg,Fe)2SiO4

### History

Egypt has long been known as a source for fine chrysolite, or peridot. These stones are formed through volcanic action deep within the earth and their history is as ancient as the fire that created them. Legend says that Cleopatra loved peridot and this stone, not emerald, adorned her jewelry.

I personally love peridot. I first began experimenting with it after a sixteen–hour–long car ride. I was guided to place the stone on my sacral chakra and within minutes I heard a slight crack and felt my back snap into place, relieving all tension. I call peridot the chiropractor of the mineral kingdom! When I first get stones, I don't like to tell my friends what they do for me because I want to see what happens to them. Out of curiosity, I gave a piece of peridot to my good friend. Strangely, within a couple of days, she called me back and said the strangest thing had happened. The stone cracked her ankle and brought it back into align–ment. The peridot is made of parts of the volcanic core of the earth. The crystals grow on this lava, and it is as if the lava is actually like the spine of mother earth. You may have heard people say that your body is merely a microcosm of all that is in the universe. In essence, the earth would be a bigger piece of that "all that is," and I believe the peridot lines us up with the spine or core of our earth, and by doing that, you can become better aligned. It is an amazing stone!

### Cayce Uses

Cayce recommended this stone to aid in depression, to quiet and calm worries, and to bring peace to the mind.

### Sample Chrysolite Reading
### 1626-1

As to stones—rather of ivory, as may be with any colored stone; preferably the chrysolite or amethyst; should be a part of that which would be about the entity—because of the very natural vibrations for the entity. For they will bring as an attunement the quieting, and the entity will find that whenever there is a feeling of physical depres–sion, physical reactions that are as dis-ease in the body, the colors in any of these natures or forms will bring qui–etness to the body; as in having about the body the chrysolite or the amethyst color, in cloth, in drapery, in hangings.

### 688-2

[It is] Well that the entity have the stones or minerals about self when in periods of meditation, or in those peri–ods when it may find itself the more easily attuned to the influences that may use the body, either in the healing forces that flow through—through its attunements, or through the visions and the associations of the entity; [have] the chrysolite or the amethyst. For the color purple should be close to the body; and the perfumes or odors as of lavender have their influence—not as in great quantity, but [in] that [quantity] which makes for attunements.

# Jade
## NaAlSi2O6

### History

Jade, or Jadeite or Nephrite as it is also known, has always been an important stone in Asian culture and mythology with a history dating back over 6,000 years to the Neolithic Age. Jade was used for tools, eating utensils, weapons, and even currency and burning jade was part of ancient burial and cremation rites for rulers. The Chinese Rabbit is said to grind jade into an immortality potion. A giant mythological bird died and transformed into jade. Chinese emperors used jade as a communication device to the gods, and believed jade was the essence of heaven and earth, the messenger of the gods. Because of that, it was carved into statues and worshipped. Confucius said jade had several virtues including benevolence, fidelity, wisdom, and sincerity.

Jade was revered in other cultures as well. Ancient Aztecs believed jade acted as the heart for a deceased person after crossing into the afterlife. Recently, there have been several deposits of jade turning up in South America—Guatemala, in particular.

I acquired a piece of the Guatemalan jade from the guys who actually discovered this new huge piece a few years ago. I put it in the center of the home to attract harmony and abundance. I also used some tumbled pieces of jade at night to help me sleep. Jade is a journey stone, so if you decide to use it as a sleep aid, you may find it will help you in other-dimensional travels. That's what happened to me. I found myself out at some ruins looking at petroglyphs. The "dream" seemed more than just a dream. There is a theory that if you are dreaming and looking out your own eyes at a scene, that means you are actually astral projecting or visiting another dimension. For me, the quality of such dreams is different, as is the case when I use jade. Try it! It is really interesting.

Jade will also bring harmony and wealth to your home when used ornamentally. I keep a jade dragon above the front door of the house to call in abundance vibrations and provide protection. I also have several

Asian carvings with good fortune emblems on them in the corners of the house.

### Cayce Uses

Jade brings a calm dignity to those who wear it and was recommended to such souls in the life readings.

### Sample Jade Readings
### 1189-1

About the entity we find unusual characters, that may be called hieroglyphics. We find jade as combined with pearls unusual in their effect upon the entity, especially in moods.

### 1189-1

The entity was among those who came under the periods of destructive forces to the *physical* structure of the school, yet later when there were the establishings of the teachings in the "city in the hills and the plain" the entity gave forth in those activities that make for the influence of the vibrations from jade and pearls in the experience in the present.

### 2506-1

Hence all forms of jade, of jewelry, of things of filigree, of peculiar odors, and the needs of such for the entity to even rest physically at times, become a part of the entity's experience.

### 2522-1

(Q) Any special jewelry that I should wear?
(A) Anything that is jade or green; not opals, however. Though these appear in the seal, they are—as self—sometimes fickle.

### Carbuncle/Garnet, Beryl, Emerald, Agate

Carbuncle is a word used to describe a precious stone. It is written about in a short story called "The Adventures of the Blue Carbuncle" in

Sir Arthur Conan Doyle's Sherlock Holmes series. Carbuncle is modernly referred to as garnet, but the term had previously been used to describe rubies and sapphires, as well, primarily because it was not until the early 1900s that ruby was correctly identified as a stone separate from garnet. In fact, the two are not related at all, yet people in ancient times could not tell them apart. It was quite a shock to discover that ruby's sister was not garnet, but the beautiful blue sapphire. Garnet is the most likely stone of all those listed above. How the beryl, emerald, and agate got into the translation is beyond my understanding.

## *Garnet*
### Mg3Al 2(SiO4)3

### History

Garnet refers to an entire family of minerals that have an aluminum silicate base. They vary in color from red to green depending on the mineral content. The word Garnet comes from the Latin word *"granatus"* meaning seed or grain. Aside from its place in the Bible, Garnet has had an important past for many cultures. Primitive garnet jewelry dating as far back as the Bronze Age (3000 B.C.) was discovered, as well as in ancient Egypt, Sumeria, and Sweden. Egyptians believed garnet should be placed inside the tomb to light the way into the afterlife, and was later to have aided Noah to illuminate his path in the ark. King Solomon wore garnet in battle for protection.

Since the Middle Ages, garnet has been known for curing illnesses of the blood and infections. It is also known to protect people from poisoning, which used to be a common concern for many people.

Spiritually, it should be given as a gift to those you love in the spirit of commitment to the relationship. It ensures long–lasting love and fidelity. The red color represents passion, not only between lovers, but passion for life and all of your endeavors.

Because of its reputation as an illumination stone, garnet can also assist you in becoming clear about a situation, or can literally light your path—as you go on trips or long journeys it will protect you. It can also assist on the journey to enlightenment by removing obstacles standing in your way.

**Agate**

**Alabaster Scarab**

**Amber**

**Amethyst**

**Angel Aura**

**Aqua Aura**

**Aquamarine**

**Arsenopyrite**

**Azurite–Morenci, AZ**

**Azurite**

**Azurite Flower**

**Bloodstone**

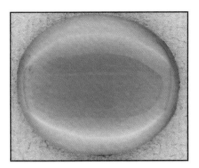

**Blue Chalcedony**

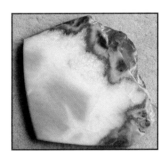

**Blue Opal**

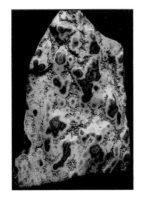

**Chrysocolla**

**Chrysolite/Peridot**

**Cinnabar**

**Coney Calcite**

**Copper**

**Crocoite**

**Emerald**

**Fluorite**

**Garnet Crystals**

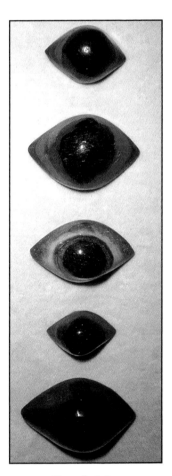

**Eye Agate**

**Gold Calcite**

**Gold–Krugerrand**

**Infinite**

**Jade**

**Lapis–My Singing Lapis**

**Lapis**

**Larimar Fossil**

**Larimar**

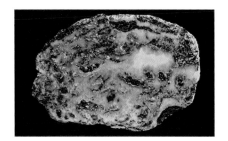

**Larimar–Volcanic Log**

**Lepidolite**

**Lithium Quartz**

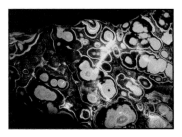

**Malachite**

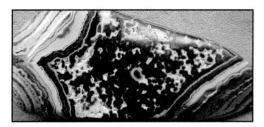

**Malachite-Azurite**

**Malachite**

**Malachite Flower**

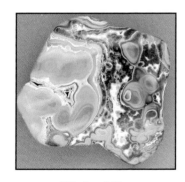

**Malachite**

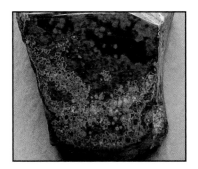

**Malachite-Azurite, Morenci, AZ**

**Mookite Jasper**

**Mookite Pieces**

**Mushroom Coral**

**Nickel Magnesite**

**Onyx**

**Opals**

**Rhodonite**

**Rhodonite Gem in Matrix**

**Ruby**

**Ruby Zoisite**

**Sapphires**

**Selenite Wand**

**Serpentine**

**Silicon**

**Smithsonite**

**Sulphur**

**Talc**

**Titanium**

**Turquoise–Bisbee, AZ**

**Turquoise**

**Turquoise**

**Vanadinite**

**Wulfenite**

Physically, it can be used to help people with poor circulation, blood disorders, or heart conditions.

I have found garnet to be the ultimate stone of sacrifice. Not only does it protect you, it will actually take on negative energy so that it will not affect you. I have had garnet jewelry disintegrate right in front of my eyes after having been exposed to strong or overpowering energies. It wraps a blanket of love and protection around you that nothing can penetrate. It is an extremely peaceful stone to carry with you and will help you sleep soundly. Energetically it is quite different from ruby, although the two are very similar in their healing properties. You would have to experiment to see which of the two you find more appealing based on the vibrational frequencies of each. I tend to be more attracted to garnet than ruby. I do not quite understand why, but I believe with ruby I feel a sense of peace, but no real attraction—as if I have already healed whatever would need to be transformed through that stone. Garnet, on the other hand, is one that I am very attracted to no matter how long I use it. I enjoy buying and wearing gem–cut jewelry in garnet, as well as carrying the tumbled pieces around with me.

### Cayce Uses

Cayce gave a reading to an entity who lived in the biblical times and referenced the carbuncle as a stone in his influence. Although he never used the term "garnet" personally, Cayce received a letter after his death from a man who spoke about the difficulty in visually distinguishing ruby from garnet.

### Sample Garnet Reading
### 5294-1

Before that we find the entity was in the Holy Land, when there was the entering in of the children of promise to the Holy Land. The entity was then of the sons of Hittites who dealt with the sons of Aaron as they prepared the garments of the priest, and the entity supplied the various stones, especially the carbuncle and the agate of that particular land.

### 531-9 Reports

Do not remember how I came to be in possession of a small stone a few months after the reading, and far from being a genuine ruby with its wine and carmine colors or tints, to me it was a "ruby" though it could have been termed a garnet because of its leaning towards pomegranate tint, which never—as some rubies have—verged into a violet spectrum.

## Row Two

### Emerald, Turquoise, Carbuncle, Ruby

Several biblical versions site the above-mentioned stones as the possible first stone in row two. Most modern versions credit it as turquoise, a stone historically known in the Middle East. Regardless, it is difficult to identify and could actually be any one of a number of stones—beryl, jade, or turquoise because true emerald is quite rare.

## *Emerald*
### Al2Be3Si6O18

### History

Emeralds have captivated people for thousands of years. The oldest known emeralds come from Cleopatra's Mines in southern Egypt. Emeralds have appeared in royal dynasties throughout the Middle East. They were one of many precious stones used in the Taj Mahal, built in the 1600s as a tribute from the grieving love stricken Shahjahan to his beloved wife Mumtaz Majal after her untimely death in childbirth. Huge emeralds adorn the crown jewels in Iran. The interesting thing is that emeralds are not as common as people think. Some come from mines in Africa, while most come from mines in Colombia, South America. After analyzing some of the crown jewels of India and other parts of the middle east, it has been determined the emerald used in these precious pieces actually came from mines in Colombia beginning in about 500 A.D. Today emerald mines also exist in Brazil, parts of Africa, and Afghanistan. The other misconception is that the green color we see in emerald is exactly as it is found in the ground. Untrue. Most emerald, and many other beautiful gemstones, are actually treated with oils to bring out their luster. Every few years, this oil treatment may need to be updated in order to preserve the stone and bring out its best light.

The rarity of the stone and the mystical allure of it could be why emerald is so revered and powerful in healing. It is one of the most powerful for physical healing. As mentioned before, any green stone provides healing support for the whole body. Emerald is special because it carries the green ray, opening the heart center. Spiritually it will help you open up to higher levels of love both for your creator and for romantic love. If your heart has been broken in the past, it will ease you into healing so you can love again.

Physically, I have used emerald to assist clients with heart problems such as congestive heart failure, and restricted arteries. One man used the stone by carrying it in his breast pocket, and when he returned for a follow-up checkup to his doctor, there was no longer any trace of his heart condition. Green stones are also used for any painful conditions such as arthritis and cancers.

### Cayce Uses

Through analysis, the A.R.E. showed the extremely high vibrations of emerald, second only to radium which is the radioactive element mentioned in part two of the book. This is a more scientific testament to the amazing healing capabilities of this stone. Other mentions of emerald were to people who used the stone in previous lives. I am sure many of us have had experience with emerald at some point in our soul's journey.

### Sample Emerald Readings
### 2431-1 Reports

The highest vibrations he has ever tested is radium at 181—the next lowest is emerald at 80. He knows nothing between 80 and 181.

### 1493-1

Such teachings were correlated and disseminated; whether pertaining to the arts, those things of a commercial nature the delvings into the earth and into the strange places for those things that might be turned into adornments as of silver and gold or precious stones—diamonds, emeralds, onyx, beryl, jasper, and all those things that made for adornment. These were the interests, these were the activities of the entity as related especially to the preparation of individuals for their material actions in those periods.

### 3657-1

The entity was among those set in charge of the preparations of the precious metals; as a carver of gold, a carver of stones—as of rubies, diamonds, emeralds and those prepared for those in authority and in power.

## *Turquoise*
### CuAl6(PO4)4(OH)8*4H2O

### History

Turquoise has been around since the dawn of civilization itself. Mining began in the Sinai Peninsula in 5500 B.C., during the reign of Egyptian Queen Zer who was wearing a turquoise bracelet on her wrist when her tomb was excavated in 1900. Turquoise was also discovered in Persia dating back to 5000 B.C., which is initially where much of the world's turquoise supply came from, so there are several myths about the stone that originated there and in other parts of the Middle East. For example, Persians believed it was considered lucky to see the reflection of the new moon in turquoise, and if the stone changed color it was a sign of bad luck or that someone was unfaithful.

In 1000 A.D. the Anasasi people of Chaco Canyon, New Mexico, began mining turquoise and used it in trade, causing it to later become an important part of most Native American cultures. The Zuni believed turquoise protected them from demons; the Apaches believed it protected them from war and helped them in battle; and the Navajo used it in their rain making ceremonies.

Turquoise gets its name from European trade markets where it is known as the "Turkish Stone" because it was such an integral part of trade in ancient times. In fact, Shakespeare wrote about it in the play *The Merchant of Venice*. Europeans believed it protected horses and their riders from illnesses and falls and that if a piece of turquoise lost its color, it was a sign that a person was ill.

Turquoise has been a part of my life since childhood. I grew up in New Mexico and Arizona and my father worked at a huge turquoise mining company in the 1970s near some of the places mentioned in the Cayce readings.

There is no doubt that turquoise is a very special stone I believe it connects you with the heavens while healing the physical body here on earth. I have used it for overall healing support because it has an unusually high vibration—much higher than other stones previously mentioned. It could be that, because it is truly the most ancient of stones, it carries the wisdom of the ages.

### Cayce Uses

Cayce again demonstrated his amazing knowledge of topography in assisting oil speculators. The areas he knew so much about are some of the same ones where he spoke about Lapis Linguis being discovered. In a letter written to Hugh Lynn Cayce, one man calls Lapis Azule turquoise. Could the stones be one in the same? The possibilities will be explored at length in the next section.

### Sample Turquoise Readings
### 195-5

(Q) You will give the condition of this land for drilling an oil well. You will also answer the following question: Is there any underlying sands carrying pay oil?
(A) There are in section 7 those conditions from the surface and in spots, where other minerals might be obtained—opal and turquoise. These could be made to pay. These will be good lands.

### 195-7

(Q) Now, on Section 7, (West Gila and Salt River Base

Meridian, Yuma County, Arizona) where does opal and turquoise outcrop?
(A) The outcrop we find is in the ridge that lies in the western half of this section, near a clump or bunch of the mesquite, and is in the quartz that shows in the ridge rather than the ravine that comes near this line.

### 531-9 Reports

12/2/46 Mr. [531]'s letter from Phila. to HLC: "Will you please tell Mr. Green [S. N. Green] that I have a lapiz azule (turquesa) stone and a small, apparently "ruby" where one that I really valued years ago has been lost . . .

### Sapphire, Lapis Lazuli

While most versions of the Bible confirm sapphire as the identity of the second stone in row two, some sources cite lapis as the true stone, based on geological evidence. There could be something to that theory based on the Cayce readings; since he was a student of the Bible, it would make sense that he would speak of those stones related to biblical times. We will discuss lapis at length in the next section because it was by far the single most important gemstone in the Cayce readings.

## *Sapphire*
### AIO3

### History

Sapphires are members of the corundum family and more common sisters to the ruby. Blue is the color most often associated with sapphire, but it can actually come in all kinds of colors including yellow, purple, green, white (colorless), pink, and brown. Blue sapphire, the most popular kind, is the carrier of the blue ray, which activates the throat and provides peace and tranquility to the planet, assists people with relieving anger, depression, hopelessness, and deep feelings of sorrow and guilt.

Ancient Egyptians associated the clear sapphire with the eye of Horus and Greeks thought it had connections with Apollo. Legend says the oracles at Delphi used white sapphire as a visionary tool.

Sapphires have graced queens and princesses throughout British history. Queen Victoria of England wore a diamond sapphire tiara; Elizabeth II also occasionally wears a sapphire studded tiara; and Princess Diana's engagement ring from Prince Charles was a stunning sapphire—not the traditional diamond.

The most famous sapphires came from Kashmir where some hunters accidentally discovered a huge deposit there in 1881, and the gems were so common it was like picking up stones on a beach.

I love sapphires and use them often in self-healing. I used them on my eyes to relieve tension following long writing projects, to calm nerves, and to bring a restful and deep sleep. Although I rarely have stomach problems anymore, not too long ago I had a horrible stomach ache and used the sapphires on my solar plexus and sacral chakras. Within a minute of placing the stones there, the pain had reduced drastically.

### Cayce Uses

Cayce never mentioned sapphires himself, instead referring to the red corundum, or ruby.

### Sample Sapphire Readings
### 2533-1 Reports

Have always been interested in precious stones—am wearing a sapphire that means a great deal to me. I shall surely get a pearl, now.

### 4341-2 Reports

I lost the watch four or five days ago in the vicinity, it is platinum, diamonds and sapphires and has [ ... ] to [ ... ] engraved on back. I have ads in the paper. Could you locate it for me and I'll go get it and try to pay a reward.

### Biblical References

"It cannot be valued with the gold of Ophir, with the precious onyx, or the sapphire."                    Job 28:16

### Diamond, Quartz Crystal, White Moonstone

This stone is another with several discrepancies as to its true identity in the breastplate. Diamond is the most common opinion; moonstone is only listed once; and crystal a few times. The argument here would be similar to that about the ruby—why is this stone called diamond here while crystal is referred to by name so many times in the book of Revelation? I believe this is also due to translation discrepancies and that it is most likely that clear quartz crystal is the identity of the third stone in the second row on the breastplate.

## *Diamond*
### C

### History

Diamond is the mineral form of carbon, source of all life on earth. Because of its links to the life force, it can work miracles on those who can obtain it for healing. At an unconscious level, even the ancients must have sensed the amazing mystical and life–giving power of the stone. No other stone in history has inspired more greed, hatred, and bloodshed, yet it has stood the test of time as the one stone above all others to symbolize the purity of romantic love.

Because of the clarity of white light brought forth by diamond, it activates the crown and connects you to the Source of all that is. It can be used in cellular regeneration and DNA activation. Real diamonds are obviously quite expensive to get for healing purposes. There is another stone called the Herkimer Diamond from a mine in Herkimer, New York, that is affordable and offers many of the same healing properties as real diamonds—although chemically they are similar not to diamond but to quartz crystal.

### Cayce Uses

It is not surprising based on the historical importance of diamond that it was mentioned over 20 times in the life readings, usually to remind people of past incarnations and assist them in realigning with life-affirming vibrations from the stone that would assist their current lives. Cayce reported the stone represents love, charity, faith, and courage.

## Sample Diamond Readings
### 1847-1

Pearls and diamonds are the stones that bring the vibratory reactions and the experiences in the environs of the entity.

### 294-51
#### Cayce's dream on Saturday morning, 12/5/25:

I seemed to be led by Gertrude. There was actually a string on me. While it didn't seem as something that bound me, but rather a feeling of security from losing my way. At times it was a cord, other times a heavy rope or chain. Others it was a rope of pearls and of diamonds, then plain glass beads. I could hear her calling me but I could never see her. I could even hear her urging Miss Gladys to get behind me and push me, and I could feel her pushing me over a hill or around a corner.

And the interpretation of what the cords of diamonds and pearl represent:

Each represents those which are the greater forces—Love, Charity, Faith, Courage—see?

### 303-31

At the top put the cornucopia—this in bright colors, with the fruit of the spirit poured from same. Here these figures would be *twelve* in number. These take different shapes, mostly as of triangles, however, or not fully round as rolled from same. These would be indicated as brilliants, or as diamonds, or as precious stones.

### 5745-1

Ye would not use a delicate object, even as a razor, for sharpening pencils! Ye would not give thy diamonds to children, nor cast thy pearls to swine!

# *Crystal*
## SiO2

### History

Quartz was occasionally used in ancient Egypt when turquoise or other colored stones were unavailable. The name quartz originally came from the Greeks who called it *krysallos*, or ice, believing it to be a hardened form of ice. Later the term was applied to all forms of crystal. The German word *quarz* may also be linked to quartz. The stones were found in relics from China's Ming Dynasty, and in pre–Columbian earrings. In the Tudor dynasty of England, Queen Elizabeth I employed the scrying, or crystal ball gazing, talents of Dr. John Dee who used a smoky quartz ball (now the official gem of Scotland) to foretell future events. Dee claimed to communicate with the archangel Enoch and developed an Enochian alphabet and writings from those discussions. He also provided the Queen with weekly astrological forecasts and served as adviser to Elizabeth until his death, always with his crystal ball near his side.

Technologically quartz has aided the advancement of man in radio transmitters and computers like no other stone.

Because of the clear colorless nature of quartz, it is a frequency-increasing stone for each of the chakra centers and will allow you to access high levels of information both spiritually and on the physical plane. Crystals are free of color vibrations, so they are open to your suggestions, which is known as programming. You can program a quartz with your consciousness to perform any activity you wish. I have some in charge of keeping my computer running properly; others run my printer; and some keep energetic space in certain rooms of my house clear.

In healing, clear crystals—also called rock crystal—can be used to amplify the effects of any other stone or healing modality that you are using by stepping up the energy and bringing clarity and peace to situations. The white color opens the crown chakra center allowing you to access higher spiritual realms and telepathically communicate with guides.

## Cayce Uses

Cayce recommended crystal for purification of the blood and spirit.

## Sample Readings
### 2285-1

As to the elemental influences having to do with the entity's experience—we find that the crystal as a stone, or any white stone, has a helpful influence—if carried about the body; not as an omen, not merely as a "good luck piece" or "good luck charm" but these vibrations that are needed as helpful influences for the entity are well to be kept close about the body.

### 275-39

(Q) Will I develop any psychic power by looking into a crystal ball?

(A) If there is ever held that only that which is of the Christ-making may be presented there. The crystal offers rather the concentration of the physical powers, and thus offers many channels for the entering in of many an influence; yet if it is held only in His name, in His right [rite?], *much* may be received there.

### 507-1 Reports

(Q) Can you tell us anything regarding this crystal sent my father from India? Do you know who sent it to him? We have the crystal ball here.

(A) But I am very certain there is a definite connection between that and his own experience, and I feel very definitely certain that it is after all what you call the looking glass. Look within it, my friend, and see the thing that has been troubling your life. If you would only understand, see that the whole thing has within it the significance. I do not think that your father desires to look within the crystal at all, but I'm sure that if he does he will see this experience that he is avoiding. It is given to him as a symbol.

**4677-1**

*After* these vibrations have been applied for at least thirteen such treatments, then we would begin applying those rays from the Alpine Light, or mercury crystal light, for the clarifying of the blood.

### Biblical References

"The gold and the crystal cannot equal it: and the exchange of it shall not be for jewels of fine gold."

Job 28:17

"He that hath an ear, let him hear what the Spirit saith unto the churches; To him that overcometh will I give to eat of the hidden manna, and will give him a white stone, and in the stone a new name written, which no man knoweth saving he that receiveth it."          Revelation 2:17

"And before the throne, there was a sea of glass like unto crystal."          Revelation 4:6

## *Moonstone*
### KAlSi308

### History

Moonstone is a member of the Feldspar group that comes from the German word *feld*, meaning field, and *spalten*, meaning split. In jewelry, it is usually seen as a soft milky white stone but actually comes in several colors including blue, yellow, orange, and green.

Moonstone is a long time favorite of psychics and mystics, and is considered a sacred stone in India. It will bring you good luck in travel and aid insomnia. It will help you see the future, particularly as it relates to relationships, and since that is very often the reason people seek psychic advice in the first place, it is not hard to imagine why it is used by so many psychically inclined people. Moonstone is also in tune with lunar and feminine energies. In the Tarot, the Moon card is about that which is hidden, or cannot be seen with the naked eye. It allows you to receive psychic information that is hidden from the regular five senses. When things are hidden or secret, this can often refer to our own innate gifts and talents. Moonstone can be used to bring those talents to the forefront to be used and appreciated.

Moonstone also helps calm emotional fears surrounding love and relationships. If you have fear around being in love or being hurt by love, moonstone can transform that. It will also soften a hard heart and allow you to feel safe. Physically, it can ease the pain of menstruation and stomach problems and help bring about a healthy pregnancy. You can also use it as a fertility stone.

### Cayce Uses

Cayce recommended moonstone to give emotional strength and feel-ings of peace to those who use it.

### Sample Moonstone Readings
### 5125-1

. . . wear the moonstone close to your body, or on your body. It will give strength, and it will keep that which is nearest to you closer to you . . .

### 608-7

(Q) Please give any advice to the mother that will assist in making for the best development of this entity.

(A) Always let a portion of the dress, either external or that close to the body, have something of *blue* in same. Keep not as a charm, but as the influences that may bring the greater force about the body, the moonstone or the blood-stone as the ornaments about the body; but those that will be found (that are akin to these) in the turquoise blue and the pigeon-blood ruby.

### 1037-1

The pearl and the moonstone, these in combination or in their setting alone, are well to have about the body.

### 1406-1

Wear the others, as of the pearl with moonstone or the like as rings or amulets or anklets; but never those upon the neck or it he ears—rather upon the extremities; for they will make for bringing out—in the experiences of those the entity meets—those very colors and vibrations that have been indicated to which the entity is so sensitive.

### 276-5

(Q) What stones have a beneficial effect on body?
(A) Opal and moonstone.

## Row Three

### Ligure/Jacinth/ Hyacinth/Zircon, Opal

In the King James Version of the Bible, the stone listed first in row three is called a Ligure, an ancient name for a gemstone with no known modern reference. Jacinth, as it is called in the New International Version, is a stone also referred to as hyacinth, a type of reddish zircon. This leads me to believe these four terms may be synonymous. Although the Darby Bible translation sites opal as the first stone of row three, I tend to believe the stone was actually the zircon.

## *Zircon*
### ZrSiO4

### History

Zircon is one of the most beautiful and misunderstood of all gemstones. It has been unjustly shunned in recent years because people get it confused with the artificial diamond CZ, or cubic zirconia. The two are totally unrelated. Zircon is found in brown and green colors naturally but can be treated to produce blue and golden colors.

Zircon has several healing properties depending on color. The clear or blue stones will help you in communication, particularly with those you love. Browns and reds are more grounding and can help prevent food poisoning or alleviate the symptoms once you've got it. Zircon of all kinds can help protect you against the forces of Mother Nature such as accidents in bad storms, lightning, or floods. A piece of zircon in your car will prevent hail damage and theft.

### Cayce Uses
Cayce never mentioned Jacinth or ligure by name. Zircon was mentioned once in a letter and Cayce mentioned hyacinth, although it was most likely the plant he was referring to.

### Sample Zircon/Hyacinth Readings
### 531-9 Reports
While I have studied about gems, all I have done is admire them—whenever I saw a zircon with its blueish-greenish tints and I looked for the "reddish" spectrum I was seeking that contrast which in reality gave the stone some life, regardless of the art of the lapidarist.

### 993-4
(Q) Please give my seal and its interpretation?
(A) . . . On either side, at the top, would appear a *bell*; or the shape, as it were, of a bell from a hyacinth rather than a *bell* of a commercial thought or of such natures.

# Opal
## $SiO_2 \cdot nH_2O$

### History
Is opal a stone in the breastplate of the high priest, as some scholars say? In my opinion, it is not. Although thin layers of opal can occur in sandstone, most of the deposits known historically have been found in other parts of the world such as Slovakia, Russia, Japan, Indonesia, Guatemala, Honduras, Mexico, and most recently Australia. I do believe this stone plays an important part in the Cayce readings, which will be discussed in the section "Stones from Lost Civilizations."

Opal is a Sanskrit word meaning *stone*. It is formed from volcanic activity and the various mineral deposits that occur within the porous holes of the stone. It has been both prized and feared by people for ages. Most scholars credit the unlucky beginnings of opal to the book *Anne of Geierstein* in 1829 by Sir Walter Scott. The heroine of the tale had a special opal that reportedly changed color when touched by holy water. In the story, the character, Lady Hermoine, and the opal she wore were both enchanted, ultimately leading to her death. Without reading the preceding volumes of the book, readers were led to believe the cause of her death was due to the bewitched opal and the reputation has stayed with the stone ever since.

My experience with opal has been quite different. I had an amazing rough big piece of black opal that I used on my third eye. The stone immediately began to relax me, and I started to feel my entire spine straighten out and adjust to the stone. You may have been to a massage therapist and had cranial sacral work done. This is a process where the therapist holds his or her hands on the back of your head, near the brain stem, and begins to slowly adjust the fluids that run along the spinal column. It is very peaceful and settling work and sets the body in a state of profound rest. If you haven't tried it, I recommend it highly. The point is that the black opal I had seemed to be doing the same sort of work, without the massage therapist. Opal is made up of anywhere from 3–30 percent water, and because of that, it is not surprising to find it aligning the various fluids of the body.

As far as the reputation the stone has for bestowing "bad luck" on people, I do not believe that at all. Opals bring whatever you are working on into your energy field to be healed and transformed. All of the lessons you came here to learn are stored in your energetic layers waiting to move toward your body, causing an illness or lesson, or waiting for you to clear the lesson in the etheric or energetic layers first before it becomes a challenge. Opal will bring anything you are working on into your field so you can work on it. This means it is a good idea to cleanse yourself and be clear when wearing opal, although not all lessons are bad! The opal may bring the abundance you've been working so long for right into your energy field. Opal combines the water and emotions with the fire of sudden change and can be a stone of amazing transformation assisting you to heal old emotions that may be holding you back and put the fire under you to get things going.

## Cayce Uses

Cayce confirms there is no ill omen that can come from using opal. In fact, he said the opal helps to control anger. Cayce referred to opal as "the change," probably because this is a stone for powerful change due to the tremendous impact it has on the emotions and the body. A stone with so much water in it is bound to affect you because your body is made up mostly of water.

## Sample Opal Readings
### 1406-1

Hence the opal that is called the change, with the moon-stone, should be stones about the body of the entity oft.

### 4006-1

(Q) Will wearing opals by one who does not have them as a birth stone signify ill omens for that person?
(A) No, no, opals will be helpful if there is kept the correct attitude, for it will enable the entity to hold on to self or to prevent those who would be angry from flying off the handle too much.

### 314-1

The opal and pearl being those minerals that will attract and influence the entity. For, there will be particularly those periods for the entity when stones or jewelry will be of particular interest to the entity; in those periods when fifteen to eighteen months have passed will this be seen in the activities of the entity.

## *Agate*
### $SiO_2$

## History

There is no discrepancy among scholars as to the identity of this stone in the ancient breastplate. Agate has played an important role throughout history. Ancient Africans used agate in fertility rites, believing it increased sexual power and strength.

Agate is quite a common stone with hundreds of varieties, yet it can have totally different energy depending on what part of the world it comes from. Agate is a stone with many multicolored layers or bands in it. You have probably seen it quite a bit in almost any store. The color and where it comes from has a lot to do with it's healing properties.

### Blue Lace Agate

My favorite kind of agate is called Blue Lace Agate from Namibia, Africa. It is a stunning pale blue with beautiful white bands. The tranquil blue hue helps you lessen emotional pain of loneliness and loss and ease depression. It also helps you gently open your throat chakra to speak your truth in the world.

### Botswana Agate

From Africa, this agate has earthen tones and connects you with mother earth. African energy is very powerful and psychically links you to the cradle of civilization. It is very helpful in easing digestive strains and spiritually, the bands create a protective energetic shield around you to keep your energy in tact.

### Crazy Lace Agate

This type comes from the desert southwest in the United States, near Durango, and in Mexico and near Ontario, Canada. Like the name suggests, this agate has crazy circular designs running throughout. It is found in earth tones such as brown, reds, and blacks. This stone will help you keep your head on straight and discern reality from fantasy. It can be used to alleviate the paranoia accompanying schizophrenia and calms neurotic behaviors.

### Moss Agate

Moss agate is a very unusual looking white agate with green or brown fernlike inclusions in it. It supposedly helps you communicate with your plants, trees, and flowers, and I have several clients who use it in their gardens. The green color and the energy of growing plants also make it a stone to attract and grow material wealth.

### Cayce Uses

Because agates of all kinds have such a calming effect on people, it is not surprising to know Cayce recommended these to certain people for vibratory reasons.

### Sample Agate Readings
### 707-1

Hence we find the agate, the beryl, should be stones with the vibrations and under the influence that the entity may find carrying an incense to the finer self for the receptiveness.

### 1397-1

As to stones—those of blue, as well as the agate should be about.

### 1401-1

The moonstone or the agate should be as an amulet, either about the neck or as a ring, or worn upon the person.

### 500-1

As to the astrological aspects, as we find, these are of specific activity. The omen the body should ever wear on the person is a Maltese cross, or a stone of the agate or amethyst—for their vibrations are the better.

## *Amethyst*
### $SiO2$

### History

Amethyst, like all the stones of the breastplate, has an interesting ancient history, and is probably one of the most popular stones of all time. Amethyst-carved necklaces were found in tombs of middle class ancient Egyptians, and it is speculated that rulers used it as a form of currency. Ancient Greeks hailed amethyst for its abilities to protect and prevent drunkenness and named the stone for the Greek word *amethystus,* meaning *not intoxicated.* According to the myth, the god of wine and intoxication Dionysus (Bacchus) was insulted and enraged by a mortal who refused to celebrate with him, so he vowed to unleash his anger on the next mortal to cross his path who happened to be a young girl named Amethyst. She was on her way to pay homage to the goddess Diana. As Dionysus released two ferocious tigers on the poor girl, she cried to Diana for help and was transformed into a piece of white quartz crystal. Dionysus was so upset by his horrible actions, he began to cry, and his wine goblet poured out on the stone, turning it purple.

Amethyst has kept its ancient reputation through the years, and I have used it for that purpose in my private practice when clients come in to discuss substance abuse problems of any kind. The high frequency of the stone and the purple hue provide the energy to uplift addictive behaviors while relaxing and soothing clients, so they can feel at ease.

Amethyst is the carrier of the purple ray, and will open your third eye and crown chakra centers. Because of that, it is a great stone to help you open up to your psychic gifts and is a great meditation tool. It can enhance circulation, ease tension headaches, and calm anxiety.

In energy work, I almost always use amethyst because it is one stone almost everybody loves and its high frequency helps remove all kinds of energetic blockages.

### Cayce Uses

Cayce gave more clues about the healing properties of amethyst than just about any other stone. He said it is to be used as a meditation aid, has ties to the purple ray, quiets the mind, eases depression, and assists those who wish to develop skills of a seer, or psychic.

### Sample Amethyst Readings
### 688-2

Well that the entity have the stones or minerals about self when in periods of meditation, or in those periods when it may find itself the more easily attuned to the influences that may use the body, either in the healing forces that flow through—through its attunements, or through the visions and the associations of the entity; the chrysolite or the amethyst. For the color purple should be close to the body; and the perfumes or odors as of lavender have their influence—not as in great quantity, but that which makes for attunements.

### 688-2

In the Mercurian forces does the entity find the wisdom of the sage, the seer, as a portion of the experience of self, rather than in the application in that which may be gained from books or from letters—but the words and the sounds and the tones and the colors. For as the vibrations and the *healing* in the amethyst, that make for the helping and aiding in individuals' assistance or help, the wisdom is balanced in those things that are founded in *constructive* forces—which it must be, in the healing.

### 1986-1

Stones—the entity should have the amethyst (the white) about self often. These vibrations will bring greater harmony, in not only body but in the mental attributes.

### 3806-1

In the choice of stones, do wear the amethyst as a pendant about the neck, as a part of the jewelry. This will also work with the colors to control temperament.

## Row Four

# *Beryl*
## Al2Be3Si6O18

### History
Because the stone beryl has been known since ancient times, it holds

an almost definite space on the breastplate. In fact, beryl is much more common than its relative the emerald. New research suggests that the "emerald" found in the jewels of ancient Egyptians were actually beryl. The difference between the two lies in the richness of the green color provided by the element beryllium, which you read about in Part Two of the book.

Beryl minerals grow in elongated shards that serve as transmitters to higher planes of existence. Beryl physically works on toxicity by assisting the elimination organs of the kidneys, pancreas, liver, and spleen. It cleanses each and provides healing support to them, particularly if those organs are overtaxed.

### Aquamarine

I have seen some scholars list aquamarine by name in the identification of the breastplate stones. While this is possible, since it, like emerald, is in the beryl family of gems, I find it hard to believe anyone could be certain as to its identity after thousands of years. As it applies to the breastplate, I feel most comfortable calling the stone by its family name, beryl.

Aquamarine is without a doubt a powerful stone. Its light-blue hue assists those who choose to verbally communicate with the spirit world and is a favorite scrying or gazing tool for mystics.

As the name suggests, aquamarine connects you with all aquatic life and the healing energies of water and the ocean in particular. It has the power to transform and heal deep emotional pain and the physical ailments resulting from that pain.

### Morganite

This is the pink form of beryl, named after banker J.P. Morgan. It has a sweet loving energy with ties to the faerie realm. Morganite allows you to be a child again and heal a hardened heart.

### Cayce Uses

Cayce mentioned beryl and its ties to ancient civilizations.

### Sample Beryl Readings
### 1719-1

These will make for much judgment to the entity, and the beryl and scarab should be a portion of the entity's dress, ever, either worn as an amulet, the ring or such, will make for a safety in the entity's present experience.

### 364-12

In this temple, we find these of large or semi-circular columns of onyx, topaz, and inlaid with beryl, amethyst, and stones that made the variations in catching the rays of the sun.

### 364-12

In this temple, we find these of large or semi-circular columns of onyx, topaz, and inlaid with beryl, amethyst, and stones that made the variations in catching the rays of the sun. Hence a portion of same became as the sun worshippers in other portions, from which there were an egress of the peoples.

### 539-2

The entity gained throughout this experience; and still may there be seen that that was laid up, of the entity's activities, in the tomb or the small granary, or obelisks yet to be uncovered in the small or first pyramids of beryl.

## *Onyx*
### SiO2

### History

Onyx comes from the Greek word *onux*, meaning fingernail. Greek legend says the Cupid clipped Venus' fingernails and scattered them along the beaches of the world where the Fates transformed them into onyx. England's Queen Victoria wore onyx jewelry during periods of mourning, and since then onyx is often worn as a stone for healing grief during periods of bereavement.

Onyx is a powerful, protective, grounding stone, keeping you stable and centered during astral plane or out of body experiences. It can help change bad habits and relieve absentmindedness. Contrary to popular belief, most onyx is not black; it is brownish orange and has bands in it similar to agate. Much of the black onyx on the market today is dyed; yet black remains the most popular color.

Aside from times of mourning, onyx is a good choice to wear during any somber occasion, such as going to court. It will help you appear humble and apologetic and will protect you from the scornful gaze of jurors.

### Cayce Uses

Again, Cayce recommended Onyx for vibration purposes, plus the ties people had to onyx in past lives.

### Sample Onyx Readings
### 2542-1

(Q) To what color, symbol or stone does entity vibrate best?
(A) The ruby and onyx, and as to colors—the radiation of colors from both the ruby and onyx.

### 873-1

For the *entity*, turning within, may aid many in making the more marvelous discoveries; for there is a whole civilization above the entity's temple; yea, even its bed, which is almost of pure gold and onyx.

### 281-25

The furnishings may be surmised from the fact that the most beautiful things from each land were gathered there; gold, silver, onyx, iron, brass, silk, satins, linen.

### Other Biblical references

"And onyx stones, and stones to be set for the ephod, and for the breastplate."                                    Exodus 35:9

"And the rulers brought onyx stones, and stones to be set, for the ephod, and for the breastplate." Exodus 36:27

# *Jasper*
**SiO2**

## History

There are just about more types of jasper than any other stone on the planet. It has a very calm and soothing energy to it that can assist you in sleeping and dreaming, settling the stomach and nerves, and grounding you to the earth.

Jasper is a stone known since ancient times. There is little doubt it was used in the breastplate of the High Priest, and in fact was used by the ancient Egyptians and Greeks in their ceremonies as well. The stone was used in ancient European times to bring rain, and interestingly, the name jasper means "rain bringer" in some Native American cultures.

## Dalmatian Jasper

As the name implies, this jasper looks like the speckled dog. It is a beige-colored stone with black spots that connects you with the animal kingdom and Mother Earth.

## Mookite Jasper

This variety comes in rich yellow and red colors with occasional beige streaks. From Australia, it will help you tune into what the Aborigines call the dreamtime, an otherworldly, extra-dimensional place where you go to gain great wisdom and spiritual strength. When I first brought this stone home and had a showing of it, people went crazy for this particular stone. There was something about it that gave us all chills. It is really powerful for those who are attracted to it. I can't help but think it has something to do with past-life connections, because some people either don't notice it at all or are repelled by it. If you think you are attracted to the Australia/New Zealand part of the world at all, you may want to get some of this and try it!

### Ocean Jasper

The multi-colored ocean or orbitcular jasper comes from Madagascar, off the east coast of Africa. This stone connects you with all creatures of the sea and the healing salt waters of the ocean. It is an excellent stone to use in meditation because it quiets and centers the mind. It will also help transform and heal negative emotions—particularly fear.

### Red Jasper

This jasper comes from Utah and carries a deep connection to mother earth. It is an excellent stone to use for grounding and the orange-red color can help you in creative projects from art to architecture. It soothes the digestion and relieves pain of menstruation. My great friend loves this particular stone and puts pieces of the Utah variety all over her house. She has very deep ties to the Native Americans of that area, as well, so I think she is somehow connected with that energy as many people are. The red variety from the U.S. has helped me with my dreams and to connect with totem animals native to our country such as wolf.

### Zebra Jasper

This stone is striped like the zebra. It comes in several varieties. One is pure white with black stripes, like the traditional zebra. This stone will help you make decisions and fine tune your opinion on tough issues. The other variety comes from Australia and has more of a sandstone base. It is brown with rusty-colored stripes.

### Cayce Uses

Cayce mentioned jasper as it related to uses in past lives.

### Sample Jasper Readings
### 5756-12

Not in the present, but we would give that which surrounds the source, place, force, that is seen here. For, the walls are jasper, the ceilings are beryl, the doors are beryl, the floors are pure gold, the light is the Lamb.

**1493-1**

Such teachings were correlated and disseminated; whether pertaining to the arts, those things of a commercial nature, the delvings into the earth and into the strange places for those things that might be turned into adornments as of silver and gold or precious stones—diamonds, emeralds, onyx, beryl, jasper, and all those things that made for adornment. These were the interests, these were the activities of the entity as related especially to the preparation of individuals for their material actions in those periods.

### Biblical References

"Having the glory of God: and her light was like unto a stone most precious, even like a jasper stone, clear as a crystal."  Revelation 21:11

"And the building of the wall of it was of jasper: and the city was pure gold, like unto clear glass."  Revelation 21:18

# Other Biblical Stones

"And the foundations of the wall of the city were garnished with all manner of precious stones. The first foundation was jasper; the second, sapphire, the third, a chalcedony; the fourth, an emerald; The fifth, sardonyx; the sixth sardius; the seventh, chrysolyte; the eighth, beryl; the ninth, a topaz; the tenth, a chrysoprasus; the eleventh, a jacinth; the twelfth, an amethyst." Revelation 22:19-20

# *Alabaster*
## CaSO4*2H2O

### History

One of the oldest known materials to ancient Egyptians, alabaster has been used for thousands of years for making the art and lining the tombs in some of the greatest civilizations the world has ever known–Egypt, Sumer, Babylonia, Assyria, and ancient Greece.

Alabaster is a gypsum–based stone that is hard to find these days in any great abundance unless you are a sculptor or take a trip to Egypt. I went to Egypt a few years ago and bought a beautiful hand–carved scarab beetle and began to use it in meditation, because I was told it would connect me with my ancient Egyptian lives. The stone provided me some amazing meditative journeys into temples I had never seen before—at least not in this lifetime. Physically, because it has a calcium base, it was very soothing to my body; in particular the skeletal structure seemed to solidify.

If you want to get some alabaster, you can buy little scarab beetles here in the states that are imported from Egypt. I had several students who meditated with these and had several similar reports to my own. One of the most interesting follows here:

"I relived a death in Egypt where I was a powerful initiate who was perceived by a particular high priest to be a threat to him. I was not yet in full awareness of who I was—he knew who I was—it was his karmic responsibility and soul contract to initiate me—instead, he chose to betray me. Part of the initiation process was learning to trust, but he trained me to trust him instead of myself. He tricked me into an underground chamber claiming it was a secret entrance to the pyramid which was where the next stage of my initiation was to take place. Instead it was a dead end underground chamber that he sealed me in. I thought it was part of the initiation. By the time I realized what had happened, it was too late. I managed to survive on scarab beetles hoping someone would find me. I couldn't "psychically" tell anyone where I was because I had been blindfolded and disoriented before being brought to the chamber. I died betrayed and despairing. No one, except the priest, ever knew what happened to me. I felt a shooting pain run up the left side of my body from my hip to my shoulder, along the ley line through my heart."

### Cayce Uses
Cayce described lives in Egypt and told of alabaster used in that time.

### Sample Alabaster Readings
### 2329-3
The entity chose not an active force other than as a demonstration in the relationships to others through the sex relations, for the preparations of the body for the new form, the new expression. For, few of those had arisen to that state in which there were the preparations so as to produce the alabaster or all white, or all relationships that brought or made for individuality and better expression for the personality of the entity throughout the sojourn.

### 254-107 Reports
The slaves were brought from the pyramid to work at home, and they erected an entrance of alabaster and faience that led to the river, and lined it with tapestries of gold and statues of Rah.

### Biblical References
"There came unto him a woman having an alabaster box . . ."                                              Matthew 26:7

"There came a woman having an alabaster box of ointment . . ."                                              Mark 14:3

"And behold, a woman in the city, which was a sinner

when she knew that Jesus sat at meat in the Pharisee's house, brought an alabaster box of ointment." Luke 7:37

## *Chalcedony*
### SiO2

### History

Chalcedony is a word used to describe a particular stone as well as a family of stones. In this section, we will explore several types of chalcedony.

### Bloodstone

Bloodstone is a dark–green chalcedony with red specks in it. Some varieties have golden streaks in them. Legend says the red specks represent the blood of Christ and when you place the stone on your body, you will absorb these red spots and they will heal you .

Of all the stones I can tell you about in this book, bloodstone remains to this day the one I have personally seen the most miraculous healings with my own eyes. This stone has the ability to totally change color and allow you to absorb the life force from it to heal. I reported on several cases in my book *Gemstone Journeys*, and continue to see more and more examples of these healings all the time.

I have some close friends who have leukemia and I gave them some bloodstone to carry with them. Within a week of receiving the stones, they were beginning to become hollowed out as they took on the life force of the stone. One of them is now in complete remission and the other is feeling well—better than he had been in quite awhile.

Bloodstone, as the name would suggest, is known for healing all disorders of blood and can also assist in circulation problems.

Another time, I was about to go out of town to work with a family who was suffering from profound grief after the suicide of two of their children. I was guided to place my favorite piece of raw, dark–green bloodstone in my pocket and carry it with me on the trip. By the end of the two–day weekend, this stone had gone from a dark green to a yellowish color. Much of the rich green had been completely zapped out of the stone, and I felt okay after the sessions, although they were extremely emotional, as you can imagine.

Through this and so many other cases of healing I have seen, I know bloodstone to be one of the very best protective and healing stones on earth. It is no wonder Cayce mentions it often in the readings.

### Bloodstone Readings
### 275-31

(Q) What precious stone sends out the most healing vibrations for my body?
(A) Those of the pearl and of the bloodstone.

### 1616-1

Do not lay aside the rosary! Have about the entity stones that are red; as the bloodstone, the ruby, or everything of that nature—in the stone but not in hangings or draperies.

### 1770-2

Hence, the bloodstone or the ruby is well to ever be about the entity, upon its body; so that the very vibratory forces of same give—with that of thought in constructive forces—creative environs or vibrations for the entity in its use or application.

### 2163-1

Hence we would wear especially the bloodstone, cut in the form of a triangle though ovaled on its edges. This about the body brings that vibration which will be beneficial; not merely as a "good luck" charm, not merely as something upon which to depend, but as an influence, a vibration about the entity.

For, each soul, each entity, has within its inner being the sum of what it has done, is doing, about its relationships to the whole. And this is the stone to which the entity vibrates. This it is a helpful force physically, an encouragement to the mental, and vibrates upon the real or inner self.

### 3407-1

As to stones—the bloodstone, to be sure, is that which will bring more harmony as to vibrations, but in all it is the mental in self that must bring harmony—whether the entity applies itself in music or art.

### Blue Chalcedony

Blue chalcedony is a very attractive light misty–blue–colored stone. It will help you ease any throat or thyroid ailment, calm nerves, and will help you get a restful night sleep. It will gently remove fears you may have about public speaking and allow you to express yourself gently when faced with conflict.

### Blue Chalcedony Readings
### 813-1

For its greater vibration, the entity should have upon its body at all periods, the blue-green chalcedony.

### 813-1 Reports

In my life reading which you gave me in February I was instructed to wear a blue-green chalcedony stone for greater vibration. Well, there doesn't seem to such a stone! The Zodiac Jewelry Company of New York who specialize in birth stones, charms, etc., advises me that chalcedony means blue and is a blue stone, that there is no such thing as a blue-green chalcedony. So now what do I do?

8/2/35 Cayce's letter in response: Now, about the stone you should wear, I don't know what to say. The reading must have meant something definite when it said blue-green chalcedony. At the next opportunity, where we have a reading in which it would be permissible, we will ask just what this is and where it may be obtained, and under what name.

### Chrysoprase/Chrysoprasus

Chrysoprase, biblically known as Chrysoprasus, is another member of the chalcedony family not mentioned in the Cayce readings. It is a light sea–green–colored stone that is very soothing to the heart. It will also calm the nerves and will help you eliminate worries about relationships and help remove fears about matters of the heart.

### Cayce Uses

For chalcedony, Cayce recommended a blue–green piece to a woman who had some difficulties with her nervous system and throat. This is not surprising since the calming blue tones would create a sense of peace in a person and calm the nerves. Blue chalcedony is light blue in color which would help to heal the throat center. The fact that he recommended a bluish–green piece suggests the heart could be affected by nervousness, as well, and the stone would have cared for that. In correspondence after her reading, she could not find a blue-green piece and apparently passed away shortly after, probably never finding a blue-green piece.

### Sample Chalcedony Readings
### 1273-1

Hence red, as the ruby—or the onyx, or the chalcedony, that may be the color as stones or things of the nature should be about the entity in its closer activity.

## *Coral*
### CaCO3

### History

Coral is one of the organic stones you will see listed in this book. Organic means it was once part of a living organism. Today, the Great Barrier Reef in Australia is the largest life form on earth. The over 137,000 square mile reef on the northeast coast of Australia is considered one of the Seven Wonders of the Natural World. Famed British explorer Captain Cook called it: " . . . a wall of Coral Rock rising almost perpendicular out of the unfathomable ocean." The Reef has proven a deadly foe of sea explorers since grounding Cook's Endeavor in 1770.

Coral has become a bit controversial in healing lately. Some feel it is not right to use because it was once a living creature. I believe in the laws of cause and effect and that every living thing has choices to make and things to experience and learn here on the physical plane. If you and I have traveled many lifetimes and learned things, it could be said that all living organisms do the same. All minerals, metals and stones are alive to a certain degree—coral even more so. In the spirit of Native American and indigenous traditions, each item that comes to you should be blessed and thanked for allowing you to use it, with the idea that it is all a part of the plans of the creator. In this light, the coral you find to assist in your healing chose to help in that way; so honor it and all will be well.

Coral is such a blessing it would be a shame not to tap into all it can offer. Because it is the skeletal remains of a carbon-based life form, coral will heal all issues relating to the spine and nervous system. Palsy's, Parkinson's disease, Muscular Dystrophy, and Multiple Sclerosis will all be aided by this natural wonder.

### Cayce Uses

Coral is one of the most important stones of the Cayce readings, mentioned 82 times. Cayce said coral would tune people in to the healing forces of water, aid in creativity, or creation, protect highly intuitive or sensitive people from unharmonious vibrations, and bring quiet and rest to the body if it is worn on the body as a necklace.

### Sample Coral Readings
### 307-15

(Q) Are there any colors or jewelry that I should wear in order to have better vibrations? If so what?
(A) Any of jewelry or ornaments that are of coral would be well; for this is—as it represents, as it is in itself of Creative Forces, or from the water itself. Red, white or coral in any form.

### 2073-2

Coral should be about the entity at all times; worn—not as a charm, not other than the vibrations of the body as related to same. Because of the very nature of its construction, and the very activity of the soul forces of the entity, this (coral) would become a helpful influence in the experience of the entity.

Through the very indications of that element as would be helpful in its experience (the coral), we find that the entity is highly sensitive to intuitive forces, spiritual aspects, spiritual imports.

### 2154-1

Ever wear about the entity rose coral. The vibrations of same, from same, may aid in the mental as well as vibratory urge to make those influences less of a disturbing nature which might otherwise become disturbing.

### 694-2

The very red stones; as of coral, that is rather of the deep sea variety, and when this is worn about the neck or about the waist—or upon the arm—let it rest upon the flesh, for it will bring quiet to the body.

### 694-2

(Q) Should the coral, as suggested, be any particular shape or carving?
(A) No particular shape, just so it is mounted so that the coral itself may be upon the flesh of the body.

Coral should be about the entity at all times; worn—not as a charm, not other than the vibrations of the body as related to same. Because of the very nature of its construction, and the very activity of the soul forces of the entity, this would become a helpful influence in the experience of the entity. Hence this we would wear about the body, but against the flesh.

### 307-15

(Q) Are there any colors or jewelry that I should wear in order to have better vibrations? If so, what?

(A) Any of jewelry or ornaments that are of coral would be well; for this is—as it represents, as it is in itself of Creative Forces, or from the water itself. Red, white or coral in any form.

### Biblical References

"No mention shall be made of coral, or of pearls: for the price of wisdom is above rubies."          Job 28:18

"Syria was thy merchant by reason of the multitude of the wares of thy making: they occupied in thy fairs with emeralds, purple, and broidered work, and fine linen, and coral and agate."          Ezekiel 27:16

## *Ivory*
### Calcium Phosphate

### History

Although it had been outlawed for several years, elephant ivory may once again become legalized soon according to the people of South Africa. Apparently the ban on elephant hunting has now caused a population explosion that is not only threatening the elephants themselves, but many of the other species of animals and plants in Africa. Because they live so long, eat so much, and wind up damaging everything in their way because of their size, lifting the ban on ivory may mean we will once again be able to use this once-prized substance. If that happens, time will tell if we can honor and respect the gift that it is, or abuse it as was once done with the poachers of the early twentieth century.

Because at this time, ivory is not a substance in great supply it is difficult to find a piece to use in healing. Like coral, it is an organic substance. It will tap you into the vibrations of Africa and connect you with the animal totem of elephant. Elephants are known for wisdom and steadfastness.

## Cayce Uses

Ivory is mentioned over 30 times the readings, primarily as part of the life readings because it is a powerful remembrance tool when recalling particular past lives. He also refers to the link between ivory and the spiritual virtues of elephant.

## Sample Ivory Readings
### 601-5

(Q) If possible, please give information as to where I can find a design of King David's seal, which it was suggested that I should wear?

(A) Make as has been indicated. It will *one* day be uncovered in Jerusalem.

(Q) Of what would it be best for it to be made?

(A) Either of ivory, coral or gold; or ivory inlaid with gold; or gold with the raised figure of the rosette and the letter.

### 900-90

(Q) Thursday morning, July 2, 1925. "I saw three elephants, one small, one larger and the third the largest of all. Cannon balls were coming out of their mouths from under their tusks. They seemed to aim the missile at a target. One elephant, the smallest, seemed to be in distress, owing to a burnt mouth, which he rubbed in agony on his ivory tusk."

(A) This in an emblematical way, as is seen oft to man, the elephant representing knowledge, power, incarnate in the animal kingdom.

### 428-13

(Q) In continuing my own work in art—

(A) (Interrupting) This should not be of the larger pieces, but more the smaller type—or miniature. And this may be done on ivory, cellulose or the like. These would be the parts to stress.

### 2733-1

Orientals, Oriental trappings—the love of these is the harking back to that experience of the entity; especially those things in carvings of ivory, and the like.

### Biblical References

"Moreover the king made a great throne of ivory, and overlaid it with the best gold."                    I Kings 10:18

"All thy garments smell of myrrh, and aloes, and cassia, out of the ivory palaces, whereby they have made thee glad."                                             Psalms 45:8

"Thy neck is as a tower of ivory."        Solomon's Song 7:4

## *Marble*

### History

Marble is sometimes called ornamental alabaster. It is an ancient stone used to line the tombs and coffins of ancient Egyptians. Today it is used to tile floors of palaces and luxurious hotels throughout the world.

Marble is calcium based and carries much of the healing energies of that element. It is soothing to our soul to be near marble because it reminds us so clearly of our many pasts in the ancient world–Atlantis, Egypt, and Greece. IT is a stone of luxury and reminds you to take care and pamper yourself. You deserve to indulge a little and marble reminds you of the regal part of your soul.

### Cayce Uses

Marble is mentioned 63 times in the readings, many of which speak of either ancient times in Greece or Atlantis, or they are more modern references to headstones from memorial companies. It is amazing to think the stones that surrounded the ancients is the same kind we use to memorialize the dead today.

## Sample Marble Readings
### 2108-1

In the one before this we find in the land now known as Grecian. The entity then in that capacity of the lover of art, and in the *abilities* of the entity many gained the understanding of that attempted to be presented in figures, in forms, in statuary, in those forces taking shape from soil, from stone, from marble, from iron, from brass, gold and precious stone.

### 779-9

In the one before this we find in the Atlantean rule. The entity ruled well, developed much, until the again forces of the entering of others from other spheres, and through the warring of the nations then in that land, the entity became selfish in that last period. The urge from this is toward those of the arts and especially of that of the work in those of stone, marble, granite, or of elemental forces in same, for under this rule some of the most beautiful buildings were erected in that plane and the entity brought much to the peoples until those destructive forces coming from the rule in the Pyrenees brought the destruction in that land.

### Biblical References

"Now I have prepared with all my might for the house of my God the gold for things to be made of gold and the silver for things of silver and the brass for things of brass and wood for things of wood; onyx stones, and stones to be set, glistening stones, and of divers colors, and all manner of precious stones and marble stones in abundance."

Chronicles 29:2

# *Pearl*
## Calcium Carbonate

### History

Pearl is another organic gem created naturally when an irritant gets into the shell of an oyster. To protect and heal, the oyster emits a secretion around it that later becomes a pearl. Cultured pearl is created when farmers purposely place a stone in an oyster and a pearl is born. It is not exactly correct to say that a cultured pearl is "man made," because it is not. It is just hastened along by man.

Natural pearls are virtually nonexistent, only being harvested in the Red Sea and Persian Gulf at this time, and yet throughout the ages, pearls have adorned the necks and heads of many aristocrats and rulers from many cultures.

Pearls bring forth energy of chastity and purity. I had a client who went into a gas station to pay for her gas. The man at the cash register was busy, so she left the money on the counter and someone took it. She had to go to court over the whole ordeal and wore a single strand of pearls to further enhance her innocent energy. The judge threw the case out and ruled in her favor. So if you find yourself in a strange legal entanglement, use pearls. They work!

Pearls are a popular wedding gift and natural pearls are a symbol of pure divine love from whoever gives them to you.

### Cayce Uses

Cayce recommended pearl to one woman who wrote later about how it affected her:

> I felt nothing and noticed nothing personally but chemical forces within me did eat a sizeable hole in the side of the pearl. I take it from that, that I absorbed some portion of it. Finally, the entire necklace became so worn I discontinued wearing it.          951-4 Reports

Cayce also said the pearl can help relieve feelings of anger and irritation because the pearl is made from an irritant, it serves to relieve irritation in people.

### Sample Reading
### 951-4

The pearl should be worn upon the body, or against the flesh of the body; for its vibrations are healing as well as creative—because of the very irritation as produced same, as a defense in the mollusk that produced same.

### 2533-1

From the sojourns of the entity in Neptune we find rather the influences of water, as well as things coming from water, area part of the entity's experience. Thus, the entity should ever keep a pearl about the self or upon the person, not only for the material vibration but for the ideal expression.

### 2533-1

Thus the entity should ever keep a pearl about the self or upon the person, not only for the material vibration but for the ideal expression. For, it will be an omen—not only because of the vibrations that it may give to self but because of keeping the even temperament, yea the temper itself. For the entity can get mad, and when it is mad it is really *mad!*

### 1189-1

The certain combinations as indicated in the pearl—which *has* been produced by irritations. Hence the ability to build resistances is a natural influence that comes about same, and not as a talisman for preventing this or that—but that the vibrations created make for same.

### Biblical References

"And the twelve gates were twelve pearls; every several gate was of one pearl: and the street of the city was pure gold, as it were transparent glass."                Revelation 22:21

# Stones from Lost Civilizations

## Atlantis

Among the greatest legacies Cayce left the world was a huge body of information about the lost continent of Atlantis. More than any other person since Plato himself, Cayce described the land, the people and the political and geographic climate of the lost civilization with such amazing detail, it has provided invaluable clues to how this land may one day be discovered.

At this point, the one thing that would honor Cayce's memory more than anything else will be the day the Atlantis myth is legitimized by a scientifically provable discovery of some of the buildings, structures, or artifacts. The A.R. E. is moving ever closer to this goal by conducting underwater explorations and by revisiting the readings that deal with each aspect of Atlantis.

## *Tuaoi Stone*

Some of the readings deal with a stone that Cayce said was used in Atlantis called the Tuaoi stone. One woman came for a reading and asked Cayce about a seal or symbol that would be helpful for her. Cayce described the Tuaoi as part of her seal. The following reading explains the stone in detail:

> For this entity, then—in the center upon a board or paper—we would begin with the stone as the light of the activities in the temple in the Atlantean-Poseidian era. This might be termed the Tuaoi stone—T-u-a-o-i. This would be a six-facet stone of the height, as to proportion, with the rest of the chart as may be indicated. The stone of the Tuaoi would be opalescent, while the light would be indicated from the top in the rays of the white light.
>
> 2072-7

The mention of such a stone nobody had heard of before, led to a stream of scholarly inquiries into the identity of the mysterious crystal. Further inquiry from (2072) resulted in Cayce providing a very detailed description of the stone:

> (Q) Going back to the Atlantean incarnation—what was the Tuaoi stone? Of what shape or form was it?
> (A) It was in the form of a six-sided figure, in which the light appeared as the means of communication between infinity and the finite; or the means whereby there were the communications with those forces from the outside.
>
> 2072-10

Cayce went on to describe the radioactive nature of the stone:

> Later this came to mean that from which the energies radiated, as of the center from which there were the radial activities guiding the various forms of transition or travel through those periods of activity of the Atlanteans.
>
> 2072-10

And he described the stone's setting and warned not to confuse it with the crystal we have today:

> It was set as a crystal, though in quite a different form from that used there. Do not confuse these two, then, for there were many generations of difference.       2072-10

Like a crystal, the Tuaoi seemed to share the transmission abilities of quartz, but potentially much more powerful—strong enough to supply central power to the entire area:

> It was in those periods when there was the directing of aeroplanes, or means of travel; though these in that time would travel in the air, or on the water, or under the water, just the same. Yet the force from which these were directed was in this central power station, or Tuaoi stone;

which was as the beam upon which it acted.    2072-10

Cayce described the original intent of the stone—as a carrier of spiritual light:

> In the beginning it was the source from which there was
> the spiritual and mental contact.    2072-10

Later, he noted that the Tuaoi was one of the aspects of Atlantis that began pure and utopian and ended in a misuse of power. According to Cayce, the stone was gravely misused, leading to the eventual destruction of the entire civilization:

> First it was the means and source or manner by which the
> powers that be made the centralization for making known
> to the children of men, and children of God, the directing
> forces or powers. Man eventually turned this into that
> channel for destructive forces—and it is growing towards
> this in the present.    2072-10

Reading recipient (2072) later wrote a letter describing her interpretation of the Tuaoi Stone:

> Regarding the "Tuaoi stone": It does not seem to be a
> gem, in the sense of something to be worn or for orna-
> mental purposes, but rather must have been a very large
> block of crystal used in the Atlantean sacred temple.

Neither this explanation nor any of the readings give a clear indication about the identity of the stone. I was puzzled about it until I had a continuation of my recurring dream one night.

> This time, Cayce and I stood in the cave, but not in the
> same chamber where the gems had been and where the
> rest of the dream occurred. He stood smiling and then
> bent down to reach for something quite large. It was a big

almost foot-high egg-shaped whitish stone. As I looked closer, it had pale luminescent rays of light blue, yellow and pink emanating from it like an opal, although no opal I had ever seen before.

"Tuaoi," he said in a whisper as he held it out for me to see more clearly.

I woke up the next day and remembered the dream. *Tuaoi is an opal*, I thought.

Remember I briefly talked about the formation of opal in that section of the book. The opal is formed from the porous volcanic matter deep within the earth. The stone is almost all water, so it is usually found near water, and the reason for the various and amazing colors it produces is because there is no set formula for it. Opal is a combination of water and whatever mineral or element content lies near it. Aside from the water content and unpredictable chemistry, it is somewhat similar to the quartz crystal chemically because both are forms of silicon dioxide, known to be excellent frequency transmitters.

In my understanding, Tuaoi is like the opal, yet made from minerals that are radioactive in nature, such as uranium or radium.

Cayce gives a clue to the identity of the stone in the following excerpt:

The stone of the Tuaoi would be opalescent . . .    2072-7

While, as always, there is no way to prove this theory, it poses an interesting question: could our dismay over opals actually be linked to a deep subconscious memory from Atlantis where we watched our beautiful God–given gifts be destroyed by greed and power?

## Yucatan

Today when someone mentions the Yucatan, you probably think about Cancun or Cozumel, yet in ancient times, it was a wondrous place with a fascinating history mentioned several times by Cayce in the readings. There was a stone known by no other name than "firestone" that Cayce mentioned, and like the Tuaoi of Atlantis, scholars are still stumped about its identity. In the readings, the area of the Yucatan is referring to a part of Atlantis:

> In the sunken portions of Atlantis, or Poseidia, where a portion of the temples may yet be discovered, under the slime of ages of sea water—near what is known as Bimini, off the coast of Florida. And in the temple records that were in Egypt, where the entity later acted in cooperation with others in preserving the records that came from the land where these had been kept. Also the records that were carried to what is now Yucatan in America, where these stones (that they know so little about) are now—during the last few months—*being* uncovered.    440-5

Some say Tauoi and the firestone are one in the same, which is possible, but I am inclined to think they are two separate stones.

## *Firestone*

Before that we find the entity was in the Persian land, among those who carried the goods from one portion of the land to another, or a caravan maker, dealing in the linens of Egypt, the pearls of Persia, in the opal, the firestone, the lapis lazuli in Indo-China, yea the diamonds and rubies of some of the cities of gold. These find an attraction for the entity in the experience in the present. Be not rather as a hoarder but use such, then, of the knowledge of such, in the study as to the helpful force in the experience of thy follow man.    5294-1

The entity came into the experience in Egypt but was of the Atlantean peoples, and interpreted in the Temple Beautiful those beauties of the temples in the Poseidia; for from there we find those great lights—opaline lights, as it were—about the entity. And these, as we find, would be those stones that to others may bring as mystery yet the fire opal would be of the stones that should be about the entity; for the holding of that fire, the vigor, that understanding that makes for purification, even though the fires of the flesh must be burned out that the glory of self may be made manifest in being a channel for the glory of the living truths to be known and experienced among others. 1193-1

## *Mexican Fire Opal*

It is my opinion, because of the area where it is found, that the firestone Cayce is referring to is the Mexican Fire Opal. In the following passage, he gives us a clue into the true identity of the stone:

. . . in the opal, the firestone . . . 5294-1

At first, it may look like Cayce is referring to two separate stones, but look again and you will see, he is merely renaming the opal. An example would be if I said to you, "Edgar Cayce, the world's greatest psychic . . . " would you think Cayce and the psychic are two different people? No, of course not. I am describing the man with the phrase "greatest psychic." In the above passage, Cayce redefines the stone opal as the firestone. He could be referring to any opal, yet because this one has ties to the Yucatan and fire opals are unique in that area, I assume he is naming that particular kind of opal. So in essence, the Tuaoi and firestone *are* the same—they are two types of the same stone.

Fire opals have been mined since the 1870s. They carry the energy of fire, which means they will help you get things started. They are great to use when you are beginning any project to breathe life and energy into these endeavors. They can also be used to aid sluggish digestion. Fire tends to get things moving, both spiritually and physically.

### Lemuria

Before that we find the entity was in that land now known as the American, during the periods when there were the sojourning of those from the land of Mu, or Lemuria. The entity was then among the first of those that were born in what is now portions of Arizona and of Utah, and among

those that established the lands there for the building up
or growing up of that civilization in those experiences;
and was in the name Uuluoou.                    691-1

Before that we find the entity was in that land now known
as the American, during those periods when there were
the changes that had brought about the sinking of Mu
or Lemuria, or those peoples in the periods who had
changed to what is now a portion of the Rocky Mountain
area; Arizona, New Mexico, portions of Nevada and Utah.
                                                851-2

While there is no mention of a specific stone, gem, or mineral from
Lemuria, there are many readings about Arizona, an area Cayce said is
part of the lost continent of Lemuria.

In the next section of the book, we will examine what some call the
most significant stones in all the readings that happen to come from
Arizona.

Could it be that these stones energetically link us to the world that
predated our Atlantean incarnations? You will have a chance to explore
this and other possibilities in the next section.

## *The Question of Lapis*

Of all the stones in the Cayce readings, none has inspired more dis-
cussion and debate than the Lapis group. Because three distinctly different varieties of the stone are mentioned, two with old world Latin
names, researchers still question the exact identity of these stones. It is
important to identify them, though, because they figure so prominently
in the readings.

## *Lapis Lazuli*
### $(Na,Ca)8[(SiO4,S,Cl)2L(AlSi)4]6$

### History

Lapis Lazuli is an ancient stone well known in Egypt for adorning the
Pharaohs' funeral masks and other religious items. Today most high

quality deposits are found in Afghanistan.

There are reports in the readings of the miraculous "singing" of Lapis Lazuli and it was something I wanted to experience for myself, so I tried it. I placed the stone next to my left ear and waited. At first I heard nothing, then I began to hear an extremely high frequency, a barely audible tone.

As was mentioned in the above reading, the sound was so weak it seemed to emanate from my own head, rather than from outside myself.

It started out like a beeping similar to a morse code, yet again, so faint I could not make out any messages; then after keeping it in place for quite some time, the tone changed to something I could only describe as a song. It sounded like a little bird singing first thing in the morning. It was quite remarkable.

As the singing grew, my hand began to pulsate and it was as if the stone began to carry a very high vibrational frequency through my whole body. At a certain point, it began to taper off and I knew the healing was finished.

The other most profound case I have seen with the Lapis involved a student who came to my gemstone healing class some time ago. I was passing around different stones to the group and the man raised his hand.

"Yes?" I asked.

"I hate to say this," the man began, "but I have to tell you I think stones are about the lowest things on the planet. I mean, this doesn't have anything special about it!"

My first thought was of sheer wonder that the man was even at the class in the first place; yet, I soon realized why he was there.

"Yes, you are right," I said, to the astonishment of the other students. "That stone you are holding has a very low vibration. There are others, though, having higher frequencies that we'll look at now."

I reached out and picked up a small piece of pure blue Lapis I had never shown to a group before and I passed it to the man. Immediately his face began to change and he "fell in love" with it.

The whole group watched as the man's attitude, demeanor, and physical appearance totally shifted right before their eyes!

Of course, he had to purchase the stone and now carries it with him to this day. He told me later that he found by putting it in a bandana around his neck so the stone could touch his throat chakra, it had totally alleviated his acid reflux, and his normal tendency to consume nearly a roll of antacids a day had gone down to none. As far as he was concerned, this was a miracle.

He also told me that he was a frequent migraine sufferer. He did not ever seem to complain of that condition much since I have known him, and while studying the readings, I came across the following:

### 3400-2

Here we find some complications—the effects of or the beginning of migraine headaches. Most of these, as in this case, begin from congestions in the colon. These cause toxic conditions to make pressures on the sympathetic nerve centers and on the cerebrospinal system. And these pressures cause the violent headaches, and almost irrational activities at times.

This passage seems to support the idea that the acid reflux may actually be linked to the migraine headaches. I shared this information with my student and he agreed, although he had never put the two together before, that the headaches had also disappeared when he held his Lapis near.

### Cayce Uses

Several people wrote in after readings to report on the healing effects of Lapis including feeling safe in the midst of danger and feelings of contentment. The high frequency singing is also beneficial to the body. Psychic development and awakening are also attributed to Lapis. Interestingly, as was stated briefly in the biblical section of the book, several scholars now believe the stone in the breastplate of the High Priest was Lapis and not sapphire, based on extensive geological evidence. So much of Cayce's work revolved around things from ancient biblical times, it would not be surprising, yet at this point, it is only speculation.

## Sample Lapis Lazuli Readings
## 2072-16 Reports

As to your questions regarding the lapis lazuli: Both my husband and I have oval stones which we obtained from Mr. Green. I sleep with mine inside my pillow case, under my pillow. There are times when I have thought I heard it singing, but apparently the "singing" is within my ear or myself for I have heard it other than when the stone is near me. For awhile we both taped the stone over our foreheads at night, but had no outstanding experiences of any center's activity being heightened. Rather, we find the psychic faculties sharpened only and when we study, meditate, and keep our trust and mind turned to Christ and God.

### 1931-4 Reports

During the fire last week quite a few men were injured by falling trees and suffered various injuries. I felt perfectly safe even though I was assigned to the hottest district! I feel that the lapis is a great protective influence. I also might state that my personal contacts in business and in social life are happy and congenial which I feel lapis is somewhat responsible for.

### 3053-3

(Q) Any color, stone or symbol for spiritual development?
(A) The lapis lazuli should be the better, but this should be encased and worn—for this body—about the waist; not around your neck.

### 3416-1

(Q) Please give my colors, stone, odors and musical notes.
(A) The lapis lazuli, worn close to the body would be well for the general health of the body—and this you will have to be careful of very soon. The lapis lazuli, of course, is an erosion of copper; but this encased in a glass and worn

about the body would be well.

### 880-2

The lapis lazuli stone would be well to wear about the body. This is as a chrysalis to be sure of copper; thus the very natures of same produce those emanations for the body in which the environ is made for keeping holy things holy, and material things in their proper relationships. For it acts as it were as a storage of energies of the inner self.

## Lapis Ligurius

### History

*Ligures* is a Latin word that refers to the Ligurians, a group of people who live on the northwest coast of Italy. Liguria borders France to the west and Tuscany to the east and lies on the Ligurian Sea. Liguria is a very old term dating back to pre-Roman times. There is a stone especially from this area called Ligurite. I have had no luck finding out anything about this stone other than the fact it existed. It is quite obscure. You probably remember in the section about the priest's breastplate that there was a stone called Ligure, which could be an old-world name for zircon. I think this is certainly something to look into which I have tried through studying ancient Latin and Greek root word stems. "Lig" usually means "tree" in Latin, and "urius" has something to do with the law. I really don't know what that would mean, except it is interesting to note the Source did mention this ancient name verbatim. It is so similar to these other words that it makes one wonder if there is something significant about zircon. The problem is the same that you run into with looking at the breastplate stones or anything else from ancient times—the language barrier and the uncertainty of topography at that time.

I thought if the zircon was a stone native to Arizona, then I might be on to something, particularly since the stone is often green. I cannot prove that it is though, because zircon is unique in that it does not contain copper and it is obviously made of the element zircon. Cayce's stone was clearly one that contained copper, was green colored, and could be found both in the areas where civilization unfolded in the Middle East, and in modern-day Arizona.

There is another stone, though, that may fill the bill and hold a key to the mystery called Linarite.

## *Linarite*
### PbCuSO4(OH)2

In addition to Ligurite, there is also a another fairly rare stone called Linarite which is a hydrous lead copper sulfate found primarily in Spain that is a distant relative to turquoise and malachite. After I began looking into the stone, I discovered there are some deposits of it in New Mexico and Arizona in the Southwest. I wonder if these were the ancient versions of the lapis ligurius stone that Cayce mentioned in the readings. When I finally saw a piece of it, Linarite looks just like azurite with malachite, yet it is chemically different and more likely to have been found in the areas near the middle east. The Source originally called it by its ancient name, which makes me think it could be the true identity of Lapis Ligurius. The reality is that this would be difficult to prove because all of these stones are so chemically similar. The real difference between Linarite and malachite is that Linarite has lead in it and will not react at all in hydrochloric acid—it is a tougher stone than malachite or azurite.

## *Malachite*
### Cu2(CO3)(OH)2

Malachite is a powerful, yet often fragile, dark-green stone found near copper deposits and usually coexists next to azurite and turquoise. It is known as one of, if not the most, powerful abundance stones on earth. The most important current deposits come primarily from the Congo in Africa and are dark green with swirling bands throughout. Queensland, Australia, and Arizona also have deposits. The Arizona specimens are much different in appearance, as are their azurite counterparts. The color is much richer and there are less banded inclusions in the stone. You may enjoy one kind more than another because, aside from appearance, the two are very different energetically as well.

### Malachite Readings

(Q) This stone contains malekite and azurite. Is the lapis linguis either of these?

(A) The azurite.                                    440-11

### Lapis Ligurius Readings
### 1931-4 Reports

Still trying to locate lapis ligurius but has yet had no luck. The names given in the readings are in the language of a century ago, says Mr. Green, and it is difficult to find them in modern books. However he is still trying. The stone I am looking for is *green* instead of the blue lapis according to the readings.

### 1931-1

For, as indicated from the influence of the lapis ligurius, there is the need for not only the copper ore, that is a part of man's *own* development in many fields, but the need for the very combination of its elements as *protection* to not only the material benefits but the bodily forces necessary for the transmission of benefits through its own physical being.

## *Lapis Linguis*

So, in this stone lapis. Lapis linguis is that one that has been in use or in touch with those whose vibrations or emanations or auras are of such natures as to have given those vibrations in the nature that any portion of such a stone may give off that which may be heard, see?

440-11

Of the three varieties of Lapis, the Linguis remains the most controversial to date. I say controversial because nobody can say for sure what it is. Cayce first mentioned it in January 1934, and since then, scholars have worked to identify the stone. Because Lapis Linguis was only mentioned specifically just 15 times during life readings, nobody knows for sure what it is (although scholars have some pretty good ideas). Today, seventy years after it was first mentioned, several New Age advocates claim *their* stone is the one used by Cayce.

Because of that, I thought it would be of interest to take a look at each of the potential candidates to discuss why they may or may not be the lost Lapis Linguis stone.

## *Azurite*
### $Cu_3(CO_3)_2(OH)_2$

### History

Azurite gets its name from the Arabic word for blue. It is a highly visionary stone that allows the user to free the unconscious mind from clutter so high level guidance can come forth, stimulating intuition. It is also used by writers "as–you–write" as an aid for clarity in the writing process, and can stimulate any type of creativity. I received a piece from a friend and keep it near my computer when I write. I thanked her for it, and reported how well it works. Again, I wonder about what we discussed in the beginning of the book—does this stone help me write, or do I just think it does? Either way, the result is the same, as far as I am concerned.

Spleen, spine, and throat are all affected by it, and it increases memory. Azurite can also ease the pain of arthritic conditions, probably because of the copper content in the mineral.

### Cayce Uses
### Readings
### 440-11

Many various characters of this lapis may be found . . . will be found in the nature where the greater portion of the azurite is evidenced in the immediate vicinity.

## *Chrysocolla*
### $(Cu,Al)_2H_2Si_2O_5(OH)_4*nH_2O$

Chrysocolla is a beautiful blue-colored stone—a cousin to turquoise, malachite, and azurite because it is found near copper deposits—with small flecks of malachite within it. One variety mentioned in the Cayce readings found in Arizona has deep royal blue tones, while the other that is mined in the Congo in Africa, is a striking turquoise color.

This stone can be used to purify the air like an all-natural air freshener. It can also clear the air in arguments, creating an energy of forgiveness and restoring trust and balance.

It is not named in the readings but is considered to be one of the possible identities for Lapis Linguis.

## *Larimar*
### NaCa2Si3O8(OH)

### History

Larimar, known as blue pectolyte in the gem trade, is a stunning blue, white, and sometimes green stone found in only one mine in the world. Discovered in the early 1970s, Larimar can only be found in the Baoruco province of the Dominican Republic, the eastern half of the island of Hispanola. Larimar was not introduced to geological circles until the mid to late 1980s, and since then has quickly become an internationally known gem, prized by psychics and healers throughout the world.

The name Larimar comes from "Larissa," the name of a miner's daughter, and "mar," meaning sea. My friend Charles Mark has been a major influence in spreading the word about the rare blue gem and was one of the first people to discover the treasure within the Domincan mines.

When Charlie first brought Larimar to the states, a psychic got hold of a piece and began to write about the amazing powers of the stone. Later it was hailed by others in the gem healing community as a lost Atlantean stone—possibly the lost Lapis Linguis stone of the Cayce readings.

After several psychics channeled the possible connections of Larimar to Cayce, Charlie decided to mention Cayce in a magazine advertisement he was running about Larimar. In passing, his mother happened to see the ad and had some amazing news for him.

**"Honey, don't you remember I told you your father and I**

rented a home from Edgar Cayce before you were born?"
Apparently, while Charlie's father was away in World War
II, the family lived in his rental property in Ohio and sent
the rent check to Mr. Cayce in Virginia Beach. Quite an
amazing *coincidence*, or was it?

Could Charles Mark have been led to this discovery through some
soul connection to Cayce himself? We can only speculate.

In this lifetime, I have loved Larimar more than any other stone on
this earth. I cannot begin to describe the profound healing to my heart
and soul this stone has afforded me, so I would certainly be one of the
first to want to conclude, as Elaine Feister did in her 1989 article on the
subject, that Larimar is without a doubt, the stone Cayce called Lapis
Linguis. Unfortunately, based on my extensive research on this project,
I have seen no evidence to support Cayce ever mentioning this stone at
all.

I do believe the stone has ties to Atlantis, though, based on the experiences of hundreds of people I have talked to personally, many who
have deep connection to Atlantis, dolphins, and the Caribbean.

When I bought my first piece of Larimar a few years ago, I remember
meditating with it and having deep and profound dreams of swimming
in the ocean with dolphins. It has such a high frequency, I lost a few
pounds over the next couple of days just because of the impact it had
on my metabolism. Then, the crying began, as the stone cleared very
old and deeply unconscious emotions. When the crying stopped, there
was a feeling of peace and healing unlike any I had experienced from
any other stone.

Now with my clients, I see this happen all the time. I will be out at a
tradeshow with the Larimar, and I love to just sit and watch the reaction
people have to it. I can watch as some people perk up and practically
run over to my table, unsure of what it is that is attracting them. Others
are totally repelled by it—although they are few and far between.

As a hypnotherapist, I do lots of past-life regressions and the people
who are attracted to Larimar, nine times out of ten, are people who
seem to have lived lives in Atlantis.

So whether Cayce mentioned it by name or not would not exclude it from being a powerful part of the Atlantean existence. In fact, I believe some pieces are energetic record keepers of that period in history and subconsciously download that information to us.

The mystery of blue pectolyte is that nobody can understand exactly what it is and why it is the way it is. I recently read a paper on it from a student who said there is only one other stone like it and that is in the Kona Peninsula of Russia. There is a white pectolyte there, but blue does not exist. In the student's samples, there was no trace of copper, a metal known to color the stones Cayce mentioned, so there was no logical explanation for the color. The conclusion was that the stone is colored by a blue gamma ray, similar to the way our sky appears blue to us, which would explain why so many metaphysically minded people have said Larimar is a carrier of the Blue Ray.

I spoke with my friend Charlie at length about the lack of copper in Larimar, and he told me that lately there have been darker green deposits found in the samples that do have copper in them. That would make those samples more related to the other Cayce copper stones.

The new theory he speaks of as to how Larimar got here is that it could be a replacement for logs or wood. I recently acquired some pieces that show both the high copper content and the remains of what could be a petrified log, hollowed out by the forces of nature and replaced with the pectolyte material.

Just so you are clear about all this stone will do for you, first, it is a deep heart healer. It brings up old emotions and allows them to energetically break free of your physical shell, so you can hold more light in your body. It heals the heart both spiritually and physically, correcting heart problems and allowing you to be open and receptive to new love. It is linked with the dolphin, an animal totem that allows you to master the art of telepathic communication and sound, and is called the broadcaster's stone because it opens the throat and allows truth to be spoken from the heart.

Who knows what will be discovered in the future about this amazing healing stone. It is an interesting mystery, to be sure, and when Atlantis rises again, we may find the definite answer.

## *Turquoise*
### $CuAl_6(PO_4)_4(OH)_8 \cdot 4H_2O$

Although mentioned extensively in the section on the breastplate, turquoise could very well have been the Lapis Linguis stone because of its chemical composition and the localities where it is mined.

There is a series of readings concerning Lapis Linguis from a man called (440). In trance, Cayce told him he was to go to Arizona and find this linguis stone and Dr. House was to go with him. Cayce wrote House a letter to tell him about the reading and encourage him to go on the trip, but for some reason he couldn't go and told Cayce to go himself, which he did on February 27, 1934.

> (Q) Where will I find this stone in Arizona?
> (A) As indicated, about the place as given—in a ranch—a hundred to a hundred and twenty-five miles north to northwest of the place. Many various characters of this lapis may be found in Arizona, as may be of other stones in the same vicinity of a semi-precious value or nature . . .

While in Arizona, Cayce and (440) apparently visited the Bisbee mines in southern Arizona. This area of the world is one I am deeply familiar with because my father worked in the turquoise mining and jewelry industry for many years in the Bisbee mines and the Kingman mines. The primary production from these mines, at least in the 1970s when we were there, is turquoise. The Bisbee turquoise is some of the most amazing in the world. It is a rich dark–blue color and has the best energy of any I have ever seen.

In one reading the Source speaks about another stone called azure, Greek for blue:

> (Q) What type of lapis would you use in the box as a sample?
> (A) Azure.
> (Q) Azurite or azure?
> (A) Azure.                                                    440-12

Could the azure stone he is referring to actually be turquoise? It is certainly possible.

## Conclusions About the Lapis Family

For most scholars, the final decision about the identity of the Lapis stones comes directly from the readings:

> (Q) In relation to the lapis, I found a 9000 lbs. stone enclosed in a glass case, etc. Is this the one referred to?
> (A) . . . As there is in the mind of the body, [440] confusions respecting lapis and lapis linguis—it has been given the lapis linguis . . .
> (Q) This stone contains malekite and azurite. Is the lapis linguis either of these?
> (A) The azurite.                                              440-11

As the Source said, azurite is the stone mentioned by name so it is most likely Lapis Linguis. Or is it? After all, these are merely the names used to describe this family of stones all related to copper.

When looking at most stones Cayce recommended, I am inclined to think about those that would have been relevant both in biblical times in what is now the Middle East, and those that are from Arizona and see which ones are common to both areas. That is why I am particularly curious if the linguis and ligurius stones could have been either different versions of turquoise, because it is a stone more likely to have been around in biblical times than azurite, and it comes in all colors of greens and blues. It could also have been the stone called Linarite, because both turquoise and Linarite are much more durable than the delicate azurite and malachite.

Again the translation of names through the seventy years since Cayce mentioned them as well as the thousands of years since terms like "linguis" and "ligurius" were even used make for a perplexing set of clues.

The other question that remains is this: why was the Source so insistent on people traveling to Arizona to get these stones? As I mentioned in the last chapter, this was an area Cayce cited as part of the lost Lemuria. Perhaps these stones were connecting people with that time and place energetically. Cayce himself was drawn to go there. There must be something significant about that particular place because it is mentioned so many times.

Yet there is a repeating theme present about Arizona which is so prevalent, I have to conclude there is much more to it than just a quest for stones. Cayce said himself over and over again that it is not the stone one should be concerned with, but the vibrations they bring to the user, so the question is posed here: What were those vibrations? Could it be a link to Lemuria? Will that civilization or any evidence of it turn up one of these days? At this point, it is merely speculation.

The quest to discover answers to the unknown has intrigued and inspired man since the beginnings of time. This mystery will continue to do so for many years to come.

# Part Four

# Vibrational Healing for Self and Others

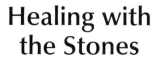

# Healing with the Stones

**A**s promised, this is the part where you will have an opportunity to select the stone, metal, mineral, or gem that is best for you.

Cayce's readings were primarily to assist people in finding out which stone or metal was right for them, usually to somehow energetically heal or support the soul vibrationally from a past-life perspective.

Unfortunately, you are not in a position now to seek Cayce's advice in this matter, but there is a way that we will explore next for you to connect with the Source yourself and see energetically which stones you should be using.

For the exercise, you will want to find a comfortable chair to sit in. I would prefer you sit and not lay down because you will want to stay awake for this process, so you can remember all that happens.

You may want to consider recording this meditation and playing it back for yourself. That way you can use it several times; since your soul is so vast, there is always more to learn about yourself each time you do this. Also, your unconscious mind enjoys and responds to the sound of your voice.

One more thing before we start. Remember to allow information to come to you however it feels best to you. You may get pictures and see everything, and that is great. You may have trouble visualizing, and if so, that is okay. Remember you can get psychic information in a lot of ways. You may get a feeling about things, or you may hear someone tell you something, or you may just have an inner knowing or gut feeling. Any way the information comes to you, just allow it to be whatever it is and know there is no right or wrong.

Let's get started now.

## Journey to Select the Stone That Is Right for You

Go ahead and sit in a comfortable spot with your feet flat on the floor and your hands placed comfortably in your lap.

Close your eyes and take a deep breath in through your nose, and blow it out your mouth. Good. Do it again. Deep breath in through the nose, and out the mouth. Very good!

Now I want you to imagine there is a beam of pure white light coming down, in through the top of your head. You can see it, feel it, or just allow it to be there. Imagine this white light is moving very slowly down through the top of your head, into your forehead, your eyes, nose, jaw, down into your neck, slowly, slowly down through your shoulders and into your arms. Imagine the light is relaxing you, just carrying away any tension and concerns you have, just melting them all away.

Imagine the light is moving through your shoulders, into your arms, your elbows, into your hands and down, down, down, into your fingertips. And imagine the light moving into your neck and down, down, down the spine, moving between your shoulder blades, through your chest and stomach down to the base of the spine.

Imagine the light continues to move down your legs, into your thighs, knees, calves, and down into the soles of your feet. Feel your feet tingle as the light passes through them and goes down, down, down into the earth.

Imagine this white light is like a waterfall just carrying away any tension and concerns you have and moving them down, down, down and out the soles of your feet and into the earth.

Imagine the light becomes so overpowering it begins to just pour out your heart, creating a golden ball of light that surrounds you by about three feet in all directions. You can see it, feel it, and just know you are totally protected by this beautiful golden light.

Imagine yourself floating inside this beautiful golden ball of light, totally safe, totally secure, feeling very peaceful and protected as if a big blanket were wrapped around you. Know that inside this golden ball of light only that which is of your highest good can come through.

Now I want you to imagine there is a doorway in front of you. Again, see it or just allow your unconscious mind to know the door is there. Open the door and walk inside a beautiful room.

As you step inside, there is a table in front of you with a comfortable chair. Look around and see what's there in the room. Feel the good vibrations of this peaceful space. You feel very relaxed and peaceful here. Imagine you can walk up and sit down in that chair and begin to notice what is on the table in front of you.

Walking slowly toward the table, you begin to see it is filled with stones and metals of all kinds—many of those you have been reading about.

Imagine you can sit in the comfortable chair just relaxing and look-ing at all of the beautiful stones and gems.

Which ones are there? Can you name them? What colors are they? Imagine you can touch them and see how they feel. Very good!

As you stare at the assortment in front of you, I want you to turn your attention for a moment to another doorway at the back of the room you are in.

Notice this doorway and now it is opening and someone is walking through. It could be a guide, or a friend, or someone who you have never met before. You may see the person, or you may just feel the warm, loving presence as they come to greet you. Imagine whoever it is has come to help you today. Say hello as they come and sit with you at the table.

Imagine you can ask this special someone to help you today as you learn which stones, gems, and metals would be best for you at this time. Know they can help you pick up to three to use today.

See, feel, or imagine the person beginning to reach out to the assortment on the table and handing you one to hold.

Reach out and, by the time I count to three, imagine you take the stone and hold it. One, two, three—you are holding the stone now. Very good!

What is it? Do you know its name? What does it look like? What does it feel like? Imagine you have an inner knowing of exactly what it is. Good!

Does your friend need to tell you anything about your connection with the stone and why it can help you at this time?

In a moment I want you to imagine you can pick up the stone and bring it inside your energy field, as if it can be totally absorbed by your body.

When I count from three, you will pick it up and bring it totally inside. Three, two, one—you are bringing it inside right now. Good!

Feel the energy of it as it travels up, up, up, through your heart, up into your shoulders, your arms and hands, up into your neck and head, and down into your stomach, into your legs and feet.

Feel the energy as it totally becomes integrated now.

Have your friend tell you the significance of this. Is this healing a past life? If so, which one? Can it aid with health issues? If so, with what?

Now imagine your friend can hand you another item from the table and will do so when I count to three: one, two, three. See it and notice what it is and go ahead and reach out to pick it up.

What is it? What does it look like or feel like?

When I count from three, you will bring it inside and into total integration: three, two, one—you are now bringing it inside. Into your heart, up into your neck, shoulders, arms, hands, and head, and down through your stomach, your spine, and into your legs.

Good! So what does your friend tell you about this stone? What is it going to help you with? Imagine you are totally aware of all it can do for you and any energetic ties you have with it from the past.

Now imagine your friend can help you today with one more item from the table. Whatever would be most for your highest good.

When I count to three, you will see the item and begin to notice what it is: one, two, three.

Notice what it is. What color is it? What healing properties does it have? Very good! Now imagine once again when I count from three you will pick it up and integrate it with your energy. Three, two, one—picking it up and feeling it as the energy rushes from your stomach, into your heart and head, your arms and legs. Feel it as you become totally integrated with the energy of this latest piece and notice how healing it is to your entire being.

Now ask your friend if there is anything you need to know about this item. What is your connection to it?

Now ask your special companion if there is anything else you need to know today about any of the three items you selected, or anything else relating to gems and stones and how you should use them.

Thank them for being with you today and imagine they can walk back through the doorway where they came from.

Now begin to once again focus on the peaceful and serene surroundings of the room one last time and go ahead and get up and walk back through the doorway where you first came in.

Now you are back where you started. Remember you are still surrounded by a golden ball of light and inside that light, only that which is of your highest good can come through.

Imagine there is a brown grounding cord of light that is coming down through the top of your head. Feel it as it moves down through your head, into your neck, and begins to travel down, down, down to the base of your spine. Imagine it is traveling down through your legs and out the soles of your feet and into the earth.

Imagine you can take all of the energy you need to feel wide awake and refreshed but any excess energy will begin now to travel through the brown light cord and into the earth.

You are grounded, centered, and balanced and in a moment, when I count from five, you will come back into the room feeling wide awake and better than you did before.

Ready? Five, beginning to come back now, four, grounded, centered balanced, three, remembering all you learned on your journey, two, knowing you will continue to process this information in your dreams tonight, one, wide awake and back!!!

# How to Give a Healing Session with Metals, Stones, and Gems

Now that you have selected the stone, metal, or gem that is right for you, you are ready to learn how to give a healing session.

First, you might want to look back at the section about chakras. Because each chakra is corresponding to a particular color, you can sometimes use the stone of a particular color to open that chakra.

For example, green stones, such as emeralds, are excellent to use on the heart center, while blue stones such as Lapis or Sodalite are great for the throat.

# Self-Healing

First you will learn self-healing. Using the stones you picked during your meditation, take them and find a relaxing place to lay down.

Next you will begin to lay the stones on your body. If they are of a particular color, ask your higher self, or inner voice, if they should be placed over the corresponding chakra. You may find the answer to be "no."

Begin then to take each stone or metal and very unconsciously and intuitively take the stone or metal and put it on your body in the first place you are guided to.

Once you have placed the gems on your body, lay there for about twenty minutes. At first, you will probably not feel anything, but after a few minutes you may begin to feel a surge of energy rush through you. When that happens, continue to rest until the sensation dies down. That is when you will know you are through with the healing. This usually takes about twenty minutes, but it could take longer.

If you cannot feel the energy, that's okay! Just allow yourself to relax and close your eyes as if you are going to take a little nap. Allow yourself to totally drift off to sleep and you will be amazed to find in about twenty minutes you will wake up feeling refreshed. That is when you know you are finished with your session.

# Healing Others

One of the most rewarding things you can do with your new knowledge is to share it with others through healing sessions.

To heal someone else, ask your higher self or intuition the question: what stones, gems, or metals does this person here before me need today to heal? Allow your mind to show you either through an internal picture, a sound, or a feeling which items are needed. You may be drawn to a particular stone, so use that! Use whatever you are guided to.

After selecting the stone or metal, again allow your conscious mind to step aside as you intuitively place the items on the body of the person you are working on. There is no right or wrong here, so just do whatever you feel guided to do.

Now, leave the minerals there for as long as you feel they should stay on the body and you can take a larger stone and give an energetic boost to the energetic bodies by waving the larger stone over the subtle energy fields while imagining all energetic bodies to become clear and open.

Use whatever stone you feel is best for this. I like to use amethyst to cleanse the aura because its soothing yet high frequency is great for removing all kinds of energetic blocks.

Gently remove the stones and end the session with a silent prayer for the well-being and continued healing of the person.

# Conclusion

### The Dream Revealed

(Q) Is it correct when praying to think of God as impersonal force or energy, everywhere present; or as an intelligent listening mind, which is aware of every individual on earth and who intimately knows everyone's needs and how to meet them?

(A) Both! For He is also the energies in the finite moving in material manifestation. He is also the Infinite, with the awareness.                              1158-14

Again, months had passed since I saw Cayce in the cavern with the treasure chests of precious gems. I thought the dream was over until one night I found myself in that space a third time.

> Cayce was standing there, humble yet of the essence of someone who has a vast knowledge within. The gems glittered as they had done so many months before, and I stood there for a moment thinking that was all there was to it.
>
> Just then, the rest of the dream was revealed as the back of the cavern blew open to expose vast open space—outer space. I found myself floating among the stars out in the universe with an incredible feeling of the connectedness of all things.
>
> The voice of Cayce was all that lingered as he said, "It is all within, it is all one." And with that, I knew the answer to the puzzle.

As we explore the readings and philosophy of the world's greatest psychic, we are reminded again and again of the magnificence of all of creation and that true power can only come from the Source within each of us.

Like the seekers who placed all their faith in a worthless statue of a bird, the true treasure could only be found by going within.

I hope the previous chapters have opened your mind to further exploration of the wonderful world of metals, elements, gems, and minerals.

> *Fulfill* that, ever, ye have promised thy God within—if ye would be true to self.                    1158-12

# Glossary

**Acid**—any substance that can act with metal to form salts and forms hydrogen when dissolved in water.

**Aggregate**—a mixture of minerals.

**Alloy**—mixture of two or more metals.

**Anodize**—to coat a metal with an oxide coat to decorate or protect the metal.

**Atomic Number**—the amount of protons in the nucleus of an atom.

**Base**—reacts with acids to form salts.

**Brass**—alloy of copper and zinc.

**Bronze**—copper and tin.

**Carbon Steel**—an alloy of carbon and iron.

**Clairaudience**—ability to receive psychic information through the sense of hearing.

**Clairsentience**—ability to receive psychic information by feeling.

**Clairvoyance**—ability to psychically see, through visions, events from past or future.

**Clay**—a sedimentary material with extremely small grains.

**Compound**—a substance with two or more elements that cannot be separated by physical means.

**Endorphins**—a group of hormones in the body that reduce pain and enhance emotions.

**Gem**—any stone prized for its beauty, hard enough to be cut and worn ornamentally.

**Igneous rock**—rock formed by hardening magma beneath the earth's crust.

**Magma**—molten lava from volcanic activity.

**Matrix**—solid matter in which rock or crystal is embedded.

**Metal**—group of positive elements, usually with a shiny surface, that is a good conductor of electricity.

**Metallurgy**—process of separating metals from their ores to make them more usable that was developed in the late eighteenth century by Slovakian chemist Josef Bachman.

**Metamorphic rock**—rock naturally altered by heat and pressure from the earth.

**Mineral**—solid naturally occurring substance with a specific hardness, color, and crystalline structure.

**Moh's Hardness Scale**—a comparative scale used to determine the hardness of various minerals. The scale takes commonly known minerals and rates them by number on hardness, and all other minerals are rated against the list to give gemologists and geologists a standard for comparison. The scale is as follows:

1 Talc
2 Gypsum
3 Calcite
4 Fluorite
5 Apatite
6 Orthoclase
7 Quartz
8 Topaz
9 Corundum
10 Diamond

**Non–metal**—any substance that lacks the properties of metals.

**Non–organic**—non-living substance lacking carbon and hydrogen.

**Ore**—a mineral or aggregate containing a valuable substance, usually a metal, that can be extracted.

**Organic stone or gem**—a once-living carbon-based substance that has hardened and formed a stonelike shape or form.

**Oxide**—compound of oxygen and another element.

**Oxidize**—any time an element reacts with oxygen.

**Precious metal**—any metal with high economic value.

**Precious gem**—any gem with high economic value.

**Processing (ore or metal)**—extracting the valuable metal or mineral from others of less value to create a pure substance.

**Programming (crystal)**—Telling a crystal at a subconscious level what its function will be.

**Refine (metal)**—to remove impurities to make a pure and more valuable substance such as a metal.

**Rock**—hard naturally forming mineral.

**Sedimentary rock**—rock formed from consolidation of clay.

**Stone**—another name for rock that has been shaped or rounded.

**Trace element**—an extremely small amount of an element required in the diet to ensure health.

**Transitional element**—precious metal.

# Bibliography

Aldersey-Williams, Hugh. *The Most Beautiful Molecule: The Discovery of the Buckyball.* New York, NY: John Wiley & Sons, Inc. 1995.

Asimov, Isaac. *Asimov on Chemistry.* Garden City, NY: Doubleday & Company, Inc., 1974.

Balibar, Francoise. *The Science of Crystals.* Poughkeepsie, New York: McGraw-Hill, Inc., 1993.

Bauer, Max. *Precious Stones: A Popular Account of Their Characters, Occurrence, and Applications, with an Introduction to Their Determination, for Mineralogists, Lapidaries, Jewellers, etc.* Rutland, Vermont: Charles E. Tuttle Company, 1969.

Betts, Gavin. *Teach Yourself Latin.* Coventry, England. Hodder & Stoughton Educational, 2000.

Bible, NIV, KJV, DARBY, WE, ASV CEV, ESV, YLT.

Broad, William J. *The Universe Below: Discovering the Secrets of the Deep Sea.* New York, NY: Simon & Schuster, 1997.

Bullis, Douglas. *Crystals: The Science, Mysteries and Lore.* New York, NY: Crescent Books, 1990.

Campbell, Dan. *Edgar Cayce on the Power of Color, Stones and Crystals.* New York, NY: Warner Books, 1989.

Cayce, Edgar Evans. *Mysteries of Atlantis Revealed: The Century's Greatest Psychic Confronts One of the World's Oldest Mysteries.* New York, NY: St. Martin's Press, 1997, 1988..

Erickson, Jon. *Marine Geology: Undersea Landforms and Life Forms.* New York, NY: Facts on File, Inc., 1996.

Finster, Elaine. *Larimar Coming to America: The Story of Larimar.* Crystal Pathways Magazine, Volume II Issue I, Summer 1989.

Friedhoffer, Robert. *Light.* New York, NY: Franklin Watts, Inc., 1992.

Harris, Stephen L. *Agents of Chaos: Earthquakes, Volcanoes and Other Natural Disasters.* Missoula, Montana: Mountain Press Publishing Company, 1990.

Hulse, David Allen. *The Key of It All: An Encyclopedic Guide to the Sacred Languages & Magickal Systems of the World—Book One: The Eastern Mysteries.* St. Paul, MN: Llewellyn Publications, 1993.

Hulse, David Allen. *The Key of It All: An Encyclopedic Guide to the Sacred Languages & Magickal Systems of the World—Book Two: The Western Mysteries.* St. Paul, MN: Llewellyn Publications, 1994.

King, Godfre Ray. *Unveiled Mysteries*. Schaumburg, IL: Saint Germain Press, 1982.

Kirkpatrick, Sidney D. *Edgar Cayce: An American Prophet*. New York, NY: Riverhead Books, 2000.

Krebs, Robert E. *The History and Use of Our Earth's Chemical Elements: A Reference Guide*. Westport, CT: Greenwood Press, 1998.

Kunz, George Frederick. *The Curious Lore of Precious Stones*. New York, NY: Dover Publications, 1913.

Liddicoat, Jr., Richard T. *Handbook of Gem Identification*. Santa Monica, CA: Gemological Institute of America, 1977.

Mottana, Annibale. *Simon & Schuster's Guide to Rocks & Minerals*. New York, NY: Fireside Books, 1977.

Patch, Susanne Steinem. *Blue Mystery: The Story of the Hope Diamond*. New York, NY: Harry Abrams, Inc., 1976.

*Planet Earth: Episode 5: Gifts From the Earth*. Metropolitan Pittsburgh Public Broadcasting, Inc. The John D. and Catherine T. MacArthur Foundation, 1985.

Schumann, Walter. *Gemstones of the World*. New York, NY: Sterling Publishing Co., Inc., 2000.

*Scientific Properties and Occult Aspects of Twenty-Two Gems, Stones, and Metals: A Comparative Study Based on the Edgar Cayce Readings*. Virginia Beach, VA: ARE Press, 1960.

Sharpley, G.D.A. *Beginner's Latin: An Easy Introduction*. Coventry, England: Hodder & Stoughton Educational, 1997.

Stemman, Roy. *Atlantis and the Lost Lands*. London: The Danbury Press, Inc. 1976.

Stwertka, Albert. *A Guide to the Elements*. New York, NY: Oxford University Press, 1998.

Ward, Fred. *Emeralds*. Bethesda, MD: Gem Book Publishers, 1993.

Ward, Fred. *Opals*. Bethesda, MD: Gem Book Publishers, 1997.

Ward, Fred. *Rubies & Sapphires*. Bethesda, MD: Gem Book Publishers, 1992.

Zim, Herbert S. and Paul Shaffer. *Rocks & Minerals: A Guide to Familiar Minerals, Gems, Ores and Rocks*. New York, NY: Simon & Schuster, 1957.

# A.R.E. Press

**E**dgar Cayce (1877–1945) founded the non-profit Association for Research and Enlightenment (A.R.E.) in 1931, to explore spirituality, holistic health, intuition, dream interpretation, psychic development, reincarnation, and ancient mysteries—all subjects that frequently came up in the more than 14,000 documented psychic readings given by Cayce.

Edgar Cayce's A.R.E. provides individuals from all walks of life and a variety of religious backgrounds with tools for personal transformation and healing at all levels—body, mind, and spirit.

A.R.E. Press has been publishing since 1931 as well, with the mission of furthering the work of A.R.E. by publishing books, DVDs, and CDs to support the organization's goal of helping people to change their lives for the better physically, mentally, and spiritually.

In 2009, A.R.E. Press launched its second imprint, 4th Dimension Press. While A.R.E. Press features topics directly related to the work of Edgar Cayce and often includes excerpts from the Cayce readings, 4th Dimension Press allows us to take our publishing efforts further with like-minded and expansive explorations into the mysteries and spirituality of our existence without direct reference to Cayce specific content.

**A.R.E. Press/4th Dimension Press**
**215 67th Street**
**Virginia Beach, VA 23451**

Learn more at EdgarCayce.org. Visit ARECatalog.com to browse and purchase additional titles.

## ARE PRESS.COM

# BAAR PRODUCTS

### *A.R.E.'s Official Worldwide Exclusive Supplier*
### *of Edgar Cayce Health Care Products*

Baar Products, Inc., is the official worldwide exclusive supplier of Edgar Cayce health care products. Baar offers a collection of natural products and remedies drawn from the work of Edgar Cayce, considered by many to be the father of modern holistic medicine.

For a complete listing of Cayce-related products, call:

**800-269-2502**

Or write:

**Baar Products, Inc.**
**P.O. Box 60**
**Downingtown, PA 19335 U.S.A.**
**Customer Service and International: 610-873-4591**
**Fax: 610-873-7945**
**Web Site: www.baar.com    E-mail: cayce@baar.com**

# EDGAR CAYCE'S A.R.E.

## Who Was Edgar Cayce?
### Twentieth Century Psychic and Medical Clairvoyant

Edgar Cayce (pronounced Kay-Cee, 1877-1945) has been called the "sleeping prophet," the "father of holistic medicine," and the most-documented psychic of the 20th century. For more than 40 years of his adult life, Cayce gave psychic "readings" to thousands of seekers while in an unconscious state, diagnosing illnesses and revealing lives lived in the past and prophecies yet to come. But who, exactly, was Edgar Cayce?

Cayce was born on a farm in Hopkinsville, Kentucky, in 1877, and his psychic abilities began to appear as early as his childhood. He was able to see and talk to his late grandfather's spirit, and often played with "imaginary friends" whom he said were spirits on the other side. He also displayed an uncanny ability to memorize the pages of a book simply by sleeping on it. These gifts labeled the young Cayce as strange, but all Cayce really wanted was to help others, especially children.

Later in life, Cayce would find that he had the ability to put himself into a sleep-like state by lying down on a couch, closing his eyes, and folding his hands over his stomach. In this state of relaxation and meditation, he was able to place his mind in contact with all time and space—the universal consciousness, also known as the super-conscious mind. From there, he could respond to questions as broad as, "What are the secrets of the universe?" and "What is my purpose in life?" to as specific as, "What can I do to help my arthritis?" and "How were the pyramids of Egypt built?" His responses to these questions came to be called "readings," and their insights offer practical help and advice to individuals even today.

The majority of Edgar Cayce's readings deal with holistic health and the treatment of illness. Yet, although best known for this material, the sleeping Cayce did not seem to be limited to concerns about the physical body. In fact, in their entirety, the readings discuss an astonishing 10,000 different topics. This vast array of subject matter can be narrowed down into a smaller group of topics that, when compiled together, deal with the following five categories: (1) Health-Related Information; (2) Philosophy and Reincarnation; (3) Dreams and Dream Interpretation; (4) ESP and Psychic Phenomena; and (5) Spiritual Growth, Meditation, and Prayer.

Learn more at EdgarCayce.org.

## What Is A.R.E.?

**Edgar Cayce** founded the non-profit Association for Research and Enlightenment (A.R.E.) in 1931, to explore spirituality, holistic health, intuition, dream interpretation, psychic development, reincarnation, and ancient mysteries—all subjects that frequently came up in the more than 14,000 documented psychic readings given by Cayce.

The Mission of the A.R.E. is to help people transform their lives for the better, through research, education, and application of core concepts found in the Edgar Cayce readings and kindred materials that seek to manifest the love of God and all people and promote the purposefulness of life, the oneness of God, the spiritual nature of humankind, and the connection of body, mind, and spirit.

With an international headquarters in Virginia Beach, Va., a regional headquarters in Houston, regional representatives throughout the U.S., Edgar Cayce Centers in more than thirty countries, and individual members in more than seventy countries, the A.R.E. community is a global network of individuals.

A.R.E. conferences, international tours, camps for children and adults, regional activities, and study groups allow like-minded people to gather for educational and fellowship opportunities worldwide.

A.R.E. offers membership benefits and services that include a quarterly body-mind-spirit member magazine, *Venture Inward*, a member newsletter covering the major topics of the readings, and access to the entire set of readings in an exclusive online database.

Learn more at EdgarCayce.org.

## EDGARCAYCE.ORG